NEHRU AND DEMOCRACY

JAWAHARLAL NEHRU

ORIENT LONGMANS PRIVATE LTD.
17 CHITTARANJAN AVENUE, CALCUTTA 13
NICOL ROAD, BALLARD ESTATE, BOMBAY 1
36A MOUNT ROAD, MADRAS 2
KANSON HOUSE, 24/1 ASAF ALI ROAD, NEW DELHI 1
GUNFOUNDRY ROAD, HYDERABAD 1
17 NAZIMUDDIN ROAD, DACCA

LONGMANS, GREEN AND CO. LTD.
6 & 7 CLIFFORD STREET, LONDON W. 1
AND AT
NEW YORK, TORONTO, CAPE TOWN AND MELBOURNE

First published February 1958

Printed in India
BY P. K. GHOSH AT EASTEND PRINTERS
3 DR SURESH SARKAR ROAD, CALCUTTA 14

NEHRU AND DEMOCRACY

THE POLITICAL THOUGHT OF
AN ASIAN DEMOCRAT

DONALD EUGENE SMITH

Assistant Professor of Political Science
University of Rhode Island

ORIENT LONGMANS
BOMBAY · CALCUTTA · MADRAS

TO MY WIFE
VIOLET

FOR all those in the West who believe deeply that political stability and democratic progress in Asia are essential to the peace of the world, I can think of no better path to an understanding of the new free Asia than an effort at sympathetic understanding of the mind and heart of Jawaharlal Nehru.

Chester Bowles, *Ambassador's Report.*

PREFACE

THE writer was introduced to Prime Minister Nehru as an American student engaged in research on his political thought. Mr. Nehru's immediate comment was, 'Well, you probably know more about it than I do'. As the Prime Minister went on to explain, he could certainly *not* be regarded as primarily a political philosopher. He is a political leader, a politician, one who has devoted most of his life to the practice rather than the theory of politics. However, we must note the fact that throughout his career Nehru has maintained a more than casual interest in theory as well. His considerable reading and philosophical bent of mind have enabled him to interpret day-to-day political problems with broad theoretical perspective.

This book is an attempt to draw together Nehru's ideas regarding democracy, and to present them in logical arrangement—a task which Nehru himself has never undertaken. It is the author's earnest hope that this work may contribute to a better understanding of Nehru and what he stands for. The future of Asia is very much in the balance. It may well hinge on the ultimate success or failure of India's democratic experiment under the leadership of Jawaharlal Nehru. The facts certainly point to the need for a clearer understanding of the man upon whom so much depends.

The study is basically an exposition of Nehru's *ideas*. But it is not thereby implied that political theories are or should be speculative and somehow divorced from the realities of political life. As Dr. Sabine has so clearly pointed out,

> theories of politics are themselves a part of politics. In other words, they do not refer to an external reality but are produced as a normal part of the social *milieu* in which politics itself has its being.*

The attempt has been made to present Nehru's ideas against the background of the situation in modern India—for it is in this context that his ideas have developed. However, it would obviously be impossible to include within the scope of this

---

* George H. Sabine, *A History of Political Theory*, Henry Holt and Co., New York, 1951, p. xi.

x

book a detailed description of all of the social, economic, and political factors which impinge on Nehru's thought. The reader's general orientation with regard to these facts must to a certain extent be presupposed.

I enjoyed the great advantage of being able to prepare this study in India from July 1954 to August 1955, and should like to express a word of gratitude for the two grants which made this possible. In connection with the Fulbright scholarship, awarded by the U.S. Department of State, I should like to thank especially Dr. Isabella Thoburn, Executive Secretary of the U.S. Educational Foundation in India, for her many kindnesses. I am also very grateful for the Penfield scholarship awarded by the University of Pennsylvania.

I should like to thank the authorities in charge of the libraries of the Legislative Assembly and the Servants of India Society, Nagpur, India, for the many courtesies which were shown me.

I owe a great debt of gratitude to Dr. Eddy Asirvatham, formerly Head of the Political Science Department of Nagpur University, and now Acting Principal of Ranchi College, who guided my research work in India. Dr. Asirvatham made many suggestions which have been incorporated in the study, and it has been particularly helpful to have the benefit of the views and insights of an Indian scholar. I am extremely appreciative of the encouragement and guidance of my dissertation supervisor, Dr. Norman D. Palmer, Professor of Political Science at the University of Pennsylvania. Dr. Palmer's valuable suggestions, especially regarding the conclusions of this study, helped me to avoid errors of interpretation on several fundamental points. Acknowledgment is made of the helpful criticisms of Dr. Holden Furber, Dr. Robert Strausz-Hupé, and Dr. Gerald Thumm, all of the University of Pennsylvania. I wish to express my deepest gratitude to my good friend, Miss Helen Weslocky, who designed the distinctive jacket of this book.

Special recognition is due to my aunt, Miss Frances Loux, and my sister, Miss Ruth I. Smith, for their cheerful performance of the task of typing the manuscript. Finally, a word of appreciation to my wife, Violet Ramanjulu Smith, who made a unique contribution to this study by introducing me to the life of her native India.

D. E. S.

ACKNOWLEDGMENTS

THE author wishes to acknowledge his indebtedness for many short quotations, the sources of which are given in the text.

He is also grateful to the Information Service of India for kindly granting permission for the use of the photograph of Mr. Nehru.

CONTENTS

PREFACE   ix

1. NEHRU AS POLITICIAN AND THINKER   1

2. CHRONOLOGY OF A QUEST   9
   Early influences: the East and the West   11
   Gandhi: ethics and action   13
   Visit to Europe: socialism and Soviet Russia   15
   The Congress: presidency and jail   17
   Disillusionment: old ideals and new questions   26
   Revaluation: humanism and the scientific spirit   31
   Achievement: independence and after   36

3. THE MEANING OF DEMOCRACY   41
   Democracy as individual freedom   45
   Democracy as representative government   49
      Popular sovereignty through elected representatives, 49;
      Importance of responsible political parties, 54; *Problems
      of political leadership*, 56.
   Democracy as economic and social equality   59
   Democracy as social self-discipline   63

4. FUNDAMENTAL RIGHTS IN THE INDIAN
   CRUCIBLE   69
   General observations on fundamental rights   71
      The background of Nehru's theory, 71; *Nehru's basic
      approach*, 75
   The right of personal liberty   77
      Conditions of disorder and violence, 78; *Individual
      freedom and social stability*, 80
   The right of freedom of the press   84
      The modern Indian press, 85; *Freedom of the press in
      the present-day context*, 91

5. ECONOMIC DEMOCRACY : THE OBJECTIVE   99
   The development of Nehru's socialism   101
      The impact of Marxism, 101; *Nehru's socialism: 1935
      and 1955*, 104

The goal of economic democracy   108
An economic structure based on equality, 109; Co-operative effort in place of the profit motive, 112

6. ECONOMIC DEMOCRACY : THE APPROACH   117
The middle way: a mixed economy   119
The pragmatic approach, 119; Production the first essential, 122; A mixed economy, 123; A socialistic pattern of society, 129
The problem of land   131
Landlordism in India, 131; Dynamic forces versus static rights, 135

7. INDIA AS A SECULAR STATE   147
The ideal of the secular state   149
Definition of the secular state, 149; Secular state essential in modern times, 153; Influence of Mahatma Gandhi, 154
India as a secular state—achievements and problems   157
Constitutional foundations of the secular state, 157; Abolition of communal electorates, 159; Progress toward a uniform civil code, 162; Caste and the secular state, 166; The question of cow slaughter, 170

8. NEHRU AS INTERPRETER   175
Characteristic emphases of Nehru's thought   177
Democracy in a changing world, 177; Conflict and balance, 179
Nehru as a political thinker   181

BIBLIOGRAPHY   185

INDEX   191

I

NEHRU AS POLITICIAN AND THINKER

THE call of action has long been with me; not action divorced from thought, but rather flowing from it in one continuous sequence. And when, rarely, there has been full harmony between the two, thought leading to action and finding its fulfilment in it, action leading back to thought and a fuller understanding — then I have sensed a certain fullness of life and a vivid intensity in that moment of existence. But such moments are rare, very rare......

The Discovery of India

CHAPTER I

NEHRU AS POLITICIAN AND THINKER

So much has been written about the bewildering puzzle of Jawaharlal Nehru that it requires no little courage to state that he is understandable. The myth of 'Nehru the enigma' is perhaps a part of the larger myth of the 'inscrutable East'. One would not wish to claim that Nehru can be easily, or perfectly, understood; he is indeed a complex personality. But when the principal facts of Nehru's background and experience are taken into account, his actions 'make sense' in terms of universally recognized human motives.

One writer pondered over the question of why the world still wonders about Nehru, when it has made up its mind quite quickly about others. Eisenhower, Mao Tse-tung, Tito, Krushchev, Nasser—'depending on where you sit, you have made up your mind. They have a political rhythm. But the world is still straining to catch Nehru's'.[1] Perhaps the answer is that in the past decade the world has witnessed the emergence of a new genus of leader, and it has not yet realized that the new political rhythm does not fit into any of the old categories.

The world has known absolutist dictators for millennia, constitutional rulers for centuries, democratic politicians for a century and a half, and bolsheviks for a generation. Today the world is confronted by a new category. It is represented by a proud Asian nationalist who for thirty years struggled against Western colonialism, and won. Yet his thinking is steeped in Western democratic traditions, and he is committed to the ideals of socialism. In international affairs he assumes that free India's self-interest (and not the West's) is his proper concern. It is hardly surprising that the new political rhythm sounds unfamiliar to the ear of the Western world.

This book is an attempt to delineate as accurately as possible Nehru's ideas about the principles and problems of democracy. What does Nehru believe about democracy? How is he trying

[1] Rosenthal, A.M., 'Nehru—Still the Seeker', *The New York Times Magazine*, December 16, 1956, p. 14.

to interpret it to India? These are the questions which are raised in this study, and when they have been answered Nehru may not appear to be such a mystery after all.

Out of fairness to the reader, it would be well for me to point out frankly the basic assumption underlying this book and to submit it to scrutiny. The assumption is simply this: that to a very large extent it is possible to discern what Nehru really believes about democracy. This immediately raises certain problems. Nehru is a politician, and is it possible to determine what a politician really believes about anything? Is it possible to distinguish and separate a politician's personal beliefs from the ideas he expresses chiefly or solely for the purpose of gaining public support? In the case of Nehru, certain factors help us to reduce this problem to what I regard as manageable proportions.

1. Some of the subjects dealt with in this study are sufficiently abstract and philosophical as to be politically innocuous. In these instances it is possible to separate Nehru the thinker from Nehru the politician. Thus, in discussing the process of the 'de-individualization' of modern man, Nehru speaks as a private observer of life in the twentieth century.[1] His discussion of the respective roles of the prophet and the leader, and other subjects, falls into this category. Conjecture as to possible political motives behind such statements yields entirely too many answers. A less subtle approach probably leads one closer to the truth.

2. Some of Nehru's election campaign speeches contain obvious exaggerations, and may be taken with the proverbial grain of salt. For example, in the 1951 campaign Nehru declared that moneyed people were using the communal political parties (Hindu Mahasabha, Jan Sangh, etc.) to divert people's attention from basic economic problems. He is reported to have gone on to make the highly exaggerated statement that communalism was the largest single impediment to India's social and economic progress.[2] Suffice it to say that no attempt has been made to delineate Nehru's ideas on the basis of this or similar statements.

3. Nehru's statements are often backed up by definite

[1] *Infra*, p. 45.
[2] *The Hindu*, October 15, 1951, p. 1.

concrete action. Nehru expressed concern over India's great land problem, and repeatedly stated that continued gross inequalities in land ownership would lead to a revolutionary situation in India.[1] This concern led him to propose two amendments to the Indian Constitution (1951 and 1954) which would pave the way for extensive land reforms. There seems to be little reason for suggesting that Nehru's statements on the subject were merely made for popular consumption, but did not reflect his real views. It would not have been necessary to go to so much trouble if this had been the case. Of course it is true that successful land reforms would also enhance Nehru's own political position, but to interpret this as his principal motive would require a considerable stretch of the imagination.

4. The test of consistency may often be applied to determine whether a statement represents Nehru's real views. Nehru's published writings and speeches go back well over twenty-five years (*Soviet Russia* was published in 1928). Thus there is considerable perspective of time from which his statements can be judged. Nehru wrote in 1936 that socialism involved a profound transformation of character, by which the acquisitive spirit of society would give way to mutual co-operation. In 1952 he declared: 'We have to aim deliberately at a social philosophy which seeks a fundamental transformation of this structure, at a society which is not dominated by the urge for private profit and by individual greed.....'[2] When the statements of the nationalist agitator, who spent most of his time in jail, agree substantially with those made sixteen years later by the Prime Minister of India, they probably represent Nehru's real views. In some cases, as in his recent statements on the 'socialistic pattern of society', there are clear inconsistencies, and these are pointed out.[3]

5. Important changes in Nehru's expressed political ideas need not, in many instances, be interpreted as inconsistencies reflecting political expediency. There were at several points in his career crucial events and experiences which largely explain the major shifts in his political thinking. Thus it would be a great over-simplification to assume that Nehru's pragmatic

[1] *Infra*, p. 134.
[2] *Infra*, p. 112.
[3] *Infra*, pp. 130-1.

approach to economic policy in 1955, as contrasted with his doctrinaire socialism of 1935, was based solely or even mainly on the desire to keep peace within his party by pacifying the more conservative elements, and thus to consolidate his political position. A long series of events, including the death of his wife, disagreements with Gandhi, and Soviet Russia's opportunist role in World War II, all combined to produce a period of disillusionment in which many of Nehru's former values were questioned. His somewhat rigid socialism was profoundly shaken at least six or seven years before he assumed political responsibility.[1]

6. Nehru is regarded by many competent observers as a political leader of unusual frankness and candour.[2] His writings often reflect feelings which most men would be at pains to keep hidden. For example, in one almost pathetic passage written in 1940, Nehru, an admirer of the U.S.S.R., expressed his shock and bewilderment at Russia's *real politik*. 'We have to remember yet again that in this revolutionary age of transition and change, when all our old values are upset and we seek new standards, we must retain our integrity of mind and purpose .....'[3] Writing in 1953 to Jai Prakash Narain, the Praja Socialist leader, Nehru frankly admitted his uncertainty regarding the methods and procedures of his economic policy. 'I confess that I have a feeling of groping forward step by step, even though the goal might be clear.'[4]

7. Nehru frequently makes public statements which are *most inexpedient* politically. For example, Nehru has roundly denounced all agitations for legislation prohibiting cow-slaughter. In a country where many millions of voters revere and even worship the cow, these statements do not reflect great political shrewdness, to say the least.[5] It would have been easy for Nehru to compromise his own convictions by taking the line that the cow is symbolic of historic Indian civilization, etc., etc., and thus should receive special protection. The most

[1] *Infra*, p. 31.
[2] Chester Bowles, *Ambassador's Report*, Harper and Brothers, New York, 1954, p. 101. Cf. Norman Cousins, *Talks with Nehru*, Victor Gollancz Ltd., London, 1951, pp. 1-2. Cf. Alan Campbell-Johnson, *Mission with Mountbatten*, Robert Hale Ltd., London, 1951, p. 45.
[3] *Infra*, p. 31.
[4] *Infra*, p. 112.
[5] *Infra*, p. 171.

plausible explanation for what he did say is the simplest one; namely, that he really believes that such agitations were based on a narrow communal outlook and prejudicial to the ideal of the secular state. Another example would be Nehru's repeated statements that he does not believe that there is any moral right attached to the ownership of property.[1] Such a statement obviously offers unlimited possibilities for interpretation and distortion by opposing politicians and propagandists. Yet Nehru has made this statement, not once but repeatedly, probably because he really believes it.

8. Recognizing the basic fact of the power struggle in all of politics, one naturally assumes that politicians will in general speak and act in a manner calculated to strengthen their own positions. This creates the problem of determining whether what they say is what they really believe. What was the nature of the power struggle in which Nehru was involved prior to 1947? The basic struggle was that of Indian nationalism against the British. Most of the issues connected with that struggle have little bearing on the subjects considered in this discussion. Thus, if the study were concerned with Nehru's theory of nationalism, one would have to probe very carefully for political motives behind his statements. A secondary struggle was that among various elements of the Indian nationalist movement itself— some conservative, some communist, some communal in orientation. From about 1940 onward, the Muslim League became increasingly important as a political opponent of Nehru and the Congress, and this fact must indeed be taken into account in assessing Nehru's statements regarding communalism. But the most important of Nehru's writings during this period came from the solitude and detachment of prison life, when Nehru was politically 'out of circulation'. He spent over nine years in jail, altogether, and for considerable periods of time he received very little news of the outside world. In such circumstances, the political motives which could plausibly be attributed to Nehru in order to explain his writings would have to be very long-range ones indeed.

9. What of the power struggle in Indian politics since independence? The significant fact is that Nehru occupies a uniquely unchallenged position. Mohandas K. Gandhi, whose

[1] *Infra*, p. 145.

unofficial political power was great, was assassinated by a
Hindu extremist in 1948. Deputy Prime Minister Sardar Vallabhbhai Patel, a forceful and effective Congress leader, died
in 1950. Nehru's prestige, which had been great even before,
was made complete by the decease of these two men. Today
Nehru has no real political rivals. There are some colourful
personalities in the ranks of the opposition parties, but the sum
total of political power opposing the Congress is very small.
Within the Congress there is not one leader who even approaches Nehru's stature. He is idolized by the masses of peasants, and to a surprising degree, by the intellectuals as well.
Jawaharlal Nehru *dominates* the Indian political scene. All of
this simply means that to a great extent Nehru is not under the
constant compulsion of circumstances to say what he does not
believe. What can be said of Nehru in this respect could not be
said of Harold Macmillan, Guy Mollet, or Eisenhower. It is
the result of an unusual, and in part undesirable, set of political
conditions. But it vastly facilitates a study of Nehru's political
thought.

The above factors have been pointed out in order to support
my assumption that to a large extent we can come to grips not
only with Nehru's words but with his thought. The problem of
Nehru as politician and thinker is not an insurmountable barrier. In the following pages we shall endeavour to explore
Nehru's thought on the subject of democracy.

II

CHRONOLOGY OF A QUEST

I HAVE become a queer mixture of the East and the West, out of place everywhere, at home nowhere. Perhaps my thoughts and approach to life are more akin to what is called Western than Eastern, but India clings to me, as she does to all her children, in innumerable ways; and behind me lie, somewhere in the subconscious, racial memories of a hundred, or whatever the number may be, generations of Brahmans. I cannot get rid of either that past inheritance or my recent acquisitions. They are both part of me, and though they help me in both the East and the West, they also create in me a feeling of spiritual loneliness not only in public activities but in life itself. I am a stranger and alien in the West. I cannot be of it. But in my own country also, sometimes, I have an exile's feeling.

Toward Freedom

CHAPTER II

CHRONOLOGY OF A QUEST

NEHRU's experience through sixty-eight years of life may well be described as a quest. It has been a quest for a political faith, and is still a quest for a better future for India. The purpose of this biographical sketch is to trace briefly the most significant events which have influenced Nehru's political thinking, and to indicate the broad trends in its development. Several important periods of his life have been summarily dealt with, because they do not throw much light on the evolution of his political philosophy. Nehru's thinking has never been static. Since 1917 every decade has been marked by important changes and modifications in his ideas and the effort has been made to cast these in bold relief.

EARLY INFLUENCES: THE EAST AND THE WEST

Jawaharlal Nehru was born in Allahabad on November 14, 1889, the only son of a prosperous Kashmiri Brahman lawyer, Motilal Nehru.[1] Nehru described his early childhood as a lonely one. The first of his two sisters was not born until he was eleven years old. The luxurious circumstances of his childhood caused Nehru later to confess:

I am a typical bourgeois, brought up in bourgeois surroundings, with all the early prejudices that this training has given me. Communists have called me a petty bourgeois with perfect justification.[2]

In his early years, Nehru assimilated the popular resentment felt toward the alien rulers, although his resentment was tempered by admiration for individual English people, including his governess and some of his father's friends. Motilal Nehru, although considerably westernized, was a nationalist 'in a vague sense of the word'.[3]

---

[1] Jawaharlal Nehru, *Toward Freedom: the Autobiography of Jawaharlal Nehru*, John Day Co., New York, 1941, p. 20. For a detailed and well-written general biography, see Frank Moraes, *Jawaharlal Nehru: A Biography*, Macmillan Co., New York, 1956.

[2] Nehru, *Toward Freedom*, p. 323.

[3] *Ibid.*, p. 20.

At the age of eleven, Nehru's resident tutor, Ferdinand T. Brooks, arrived, and in course of time influenced him greatly. Brooks's influence was exerted in two diverse fields, theosophy and science.[1] The boy was attracted to theosophy and became a member of the Theosophical Society at the age of thirteen. Theosophy proved to be a passing fancy for Nehru, but science and the scientific method became a constant and dominant theme in his mature life philosophy. It was in a little rigged-up laboratory, and under Brooks's direction, that Nehru was initiated into the mysteries of science.

The boy's interest in current events was stimulated by the Boer War, and he began to read the newspapers with great interest. Later, news of the Russo-Japanese War affected Nehru in the same way that it affected all of Asia, and the boy was caught up in nationalist ideas, in dreams of freedom from the domination of Europe.[2] In 1905, at the age of fifteen, Nehru was taken to England by his parents, and began his studies at Harrow. His interest in politics and international affairs grew and so did his nationalism. He read several volumes on Garibaldi.

> Visions of similar deeds in India came before me, of a gallant fight for freedom, and in my mind India and Italy got strangely mixed together.[3]

In 1907 Nehru entered Trinity College, Cambridge, and chose the science course—chemistry, geology and botany being his subjects. As his intellectual horizons widened, he gradually assumed a fashionable sophistication.[4] Nehru was influenced by his scientific studies in the university, and caught something of the easy optimism of the science of the nineteenth and early twentieth centuries.

For several years after 1907 the Indian political scene was one of unrest, and Nehru's sympathies lay with Tilak and his revolutionary Extremist party.[5] Meredith Townsend's *Asia and Europe* exercised much influence on his political thinking. Nehru left Cambridge in 1910 after taking his degree, and spent the next two years studying law in London. He was not

[1] *Ibid.*, pp. 27-9.
[2] *Ibid.*, pp. 29-30.
[3] *Ibid.*, p. 32.
[4] *Loc. cit.*
[5] *Ibid.*, pp. 34-5.

greatly interested in law. In fact, the decision that he prepare
for that profession had been made largely by his parents. During
this period Nehru felt vaguely attracted to the Fabians and
socialistic ideas, more as an intellectual fad than anything else.[1]
In 1912 he was called to the Bar, and shortly thereafter he
returned to India. Regarding the permanent impression which
England made on his life, Nehru later wrote:

> Personally, I owe too much to England in my mental make-up
> ever to feel wholly alien to her. And, do what I will, I cannot get
> rid of the habits of mind, and the standards and ways of judging
> other countries as well as life generally, which I acquired at
> school and college in England.[2]

Although he later regarded himself as 'a queer mixture of the
East and the West', he conceded that 'my thoughts and ap-
proach to life are more akin to what is called Western than
Eastern'.[3]

GANDHI: ETHICS AND ACTION

Having joined the United Provinces High Court, Nehru
found the legal profession exceedingly uninteresting. He joined
the Indian National Congress and participated in its sporadic
agitations against the maltreatment of Indians overseas. World
War I brought increased interest in international affairs, but
it did not otherwise affect Nehru's life greatly. By 1916 the
nationalist movement was revitalized, and Nehru joined Mrs
Besant's Home Rule League. During these years Nehru continued to favour Tilak's position in his political sympathies. He
was tired of the endless talk of the Moderates, and wanted to
embark on a course of action toward the goal of complete
independence.

His first meeting with Gandhi was in 1916 at the Lucknow
Congress. Nehru and the other young men admired him for
his great struggle in South Africa, but still to most of them
Gandhi seemed 'very distant and different and unpolitical'.[4]
During most of this period Nehru was a 'pure nationalist',
his vague socialist ideas of college days having been submerged
in ardent patriotism. Nevertheless, fresh reading awakened

[1] *Ibid.*, p. 38.
[2] *Ibid.*, p. 266.
[3] *Ibid.*, p. 353.
[4] *Ibid.*, p. 44.

these ideas, which he later described as 'more humanitarian and utopian than scientific'.[1] He read Bertrand Russell's books with great interest during the war years and after. Nehru was married to Kamala Kaul in 1916 and their daughter, Indira, was born the following year. In 1919 Mahatma Gandhi started his *satyagraha* movement, and Nehru took his place in the ranks to defy the Rowlatt Act and other repressive measures.

The following year Nehru had an experience of prime importance, which changed his mental outlook profoundly. He later described himself as being at that time 'totally ignorant of labour conditions in factories or fields, and my political outlook was entirely bourgeois'.[2] By an unusual set of circumstances Nehru came into contact with the *kisan* (peasant) movement in Oudh. He spent three days in the villages, listening to the *kisans*' description of their oppressed condition, and this experience marked a turning point in Nehru's life.

> Looking at them and their misery and overflowing gratitude, I was filled with shame and sorrow — shame at my own easy-going and comfortable life and our petty politics of the city which ignored this vast multitude of semi-naked sons and daughters of India. A new picture of India seemed to rise before me, naked, starving, crushed, and utterly miserable.[3]

The experience with the *kisans* indicated to Nehru the degree to which the nationalist movement had been cut off from the life of the masses. This experience coincided with Gandhi's rise to prominence in the Congress, and his emphasis further strengthened Nehru's consciousness of peasant India.

Gandhi's non-cooperation movement got under way on a large scale in 1921, and Nehru underwent his first imprisonment in December of that year. He was released after three months, only to be re-arrested six weeks later, and returned to Lucknow District Jail. His second term lasted until January 1923. Meanwhile Gandhi had suspended the civil disobedience movement, to the consternation of Nehru and many others. The nationalist movement lost its impetus, and the Congress settled back once more to its routine programme. Nehru became All-India Congress General Secretary, and meanwhile for two

[1] *Loc. cit.*
[2] *Ibid.*, p. 54.
[3] *Ibid.*, pp. 56-7.

years served as chairman of the board of Allahabad municipality. He was not happy in the latter capacity, as he found that the 'steel frame' of British administration prevented any radical change or new development.[1]

What was Gandhi's influence upon Nehru during this period? Gandhi's continual stress on the religious and spiritual side of his movement was somewhat incomprehensible to him. When non-cooperation was at white heat there was an atmosphere of revivalism about it, and Gandhi seemed to encourage this. Nehru, with his modern, scientific and rational approach to life, simply did not speak the same language as Gandhi.

> But we felt that we knew him quite well enough to realize that he was a great and unique man and a glorious leader, and having put our faith in him, we gave him an almost blank cheque, for the time being at least.[2]

But even in religion Gandhi's influence was felt, and Nehru later stated that he had come 'nearer to a religious frame of mind in 1921 than at any other time since my early boyhood. Even so I did not come very near'.[3]

It was the moral and ethical side of Gandhi's *satyagraha* that held the greater appeal. Nehru did not accept non-violence as an absolute creed but he became convinced that, against the background of India's traditions, it was the right policy to follow. Gandhi's continuous insistence on the necessity of worthy means being used to attain worthy ends deeply influenced him. Gandhi's abhorrence of machinery and modern civilization had no effect on Nehru whatever, except to convince him and others that such ideas would have to be firmly dealt with when independence was attained.

VISIT TO EUROPE: SOCIALISM AND SOVIET RUSSIA

In March 1926 Nehru returned to Europe, after an absence of over thirteen years. This visit, which lengthened out to a year and nine months, may be considered a definite turning-point in the development of his political thinking. Up to this time, nationalism had been his principal theme, and indeed, it continued to be of very great importance right up to 1947,

[1] Nehru, *Toward Freedom*, p. 118.
[2] *Ibid.*, p. 72.
[3] *Loc. cit.*

and after. Nehru's nationalism was naturally very intense during the non-cooperation movement of 1921-22. But the extended stay in Europe gave him a better perspective of Indian problems against the broader background of the world situation. Furthermore, he was brought into personal contact with a number of socialists, and his earlier vague attraction toward socialism was sharpened. Shortly after his arrival in Switzerland, the General Strike broke out in England. Several months after the collapse of the strike he visited Derbyshire, and saw 'class justice' being wrought at the expense of the miners.

He attended the Congress of Oppressed Nationalities held in Brussels, as the representative of the Indian National Congress. There were many left-wing labour organizations from all parts of the world represented in the conference. The Brussels Congress, in which communists played an important role, revealed to Nehru the inner conflicts of European labour. He was impressed by communism.

> So I turned inevitably with good will toward communism, for, whatever its faults, it was at least not hypocritical and not imperialistic. It was not a doctrinal adherence, as I did not know much about the fine points of communism, my acquaintance being limited at the time to its broad features. These attracted me, as also the tremendous changes taking place in Russia.[1]

Nevertheless, communists personally often annoyed him by their methods, which he regarded as dictatorial and vulgar.

In November 1927 Nehru made a brief visit to Russia to see for himself these 'tremendous changes'. He wrote several articles which appeared in Indian newspapers, and these were later published in book form.[2] In these articles Nehru showed cautious and discerning judgment in evaluating what was happening in Soviet Russia. While inspecting a prison on the outskirts of Moscow, Nehru sensed that 'the whole prison was more or less of a show place, specially meant for the edification of visitors'.[3] Nehru admired the progressive outlook and mentality of the prison officials, even if all prisons might not be like the one he saw. But Nehru cautioned his readers to remember

[1] *Ibid.*, p. 126.
[2] Jawaharlal Nehru, *Soviet Russia: Some Random Sketches and Impressions,* Chetana Ltd., Bombay, 1929.
[3] *Ibid.*, p. 70.

that the humane principles of the general criminal law did not apply to political prisoners, who were considered to be enemies of society. Those who deviated from the Party could expect no mercy from the State. 'The Soviet Government has a special and a ruthless way of treating its political opponents and all those whom it may suspect of counter-revolutionary activities.'[1] It is quite evident that Nehru was not swept off his feet by the claims of Russian communism.

The general tone of his report, however, was one of admiration. He summed up his conclusions in this tentative fashion:

> I shall not venture to pass judgment or to give final opinions. I too am impressionable and I must confess that the impressions I carried back with me from Moscow were very favourable and all my reading has confirmed these impressions, although there is much that I do not understand and much that I do not like or admire.[2]

The Nehru who returned to India in December 1927 was a considerably different individual, politically, from the Nehru who had departed for Europe twenty-one months earlier.

> My outlook was wider, and nationalism by itself seemed to me definitely a narrow and insufficient creed. Political freedom, indedendence, were no doubt essential, but they were steps only in the right direction; without social freedom and a socialistic structure of society and the State, neither the country nor the individual could develop much.[3]

It is significant that Nehru had not committed himself to any definite social ideology until the age of thirty-eight.

Nationalism continued to be a prominent thread in the fabric of Nehru's political thinking. This was inevitable, as all of his thinking was done in the context of the struggle for independence. Socialism was still largely a theoretical issue, until independence would be attained. Nevertheless, from 1927 onward, and through the 1930s, socialism increasingly provided the basic pattern for the fabric, into which the older thread of nationalism was woven.

THE CONGRESS: PRESIDENCY AND JAIL

Upon his return to India, Nehru plunged into the work of

---

[1] *Ibid.*, p. 76.
[2] *Ibid.*, pp. 33-4.
[3] Nehru, *Toward Freedom*, p. 128.

the National Congress with enthusiasm. He travelled a great deal and delivered many public addresses. He later recorded: 'Everywhere I spoke on political independence and social freedom and made the former a step toward attainment of the latter.'[1] He became acutely aware of the narrowness of the nationalism of many of his colleagues, and made a concerted effort to spread the ideology of socialism among them. In December 1928 Nehru participated in the All-India Trade-Union Congress held at Jharia. Although a newcomer to Indian trade-union work, he had attained a measure of popularity with the workers which was evidenced by his being elected *in absentia* president of the Trade-Union Congress.

Motilal Nehru was then president of the Indian National Congress, and the following year this honour was passed on to Jawaharlal Nehru. Nehru presided over the Congress at the relatively young age of forty, and had the distinction of being re-elected president of the Trade-Union Congress as well. He hoped to bring the two movements closer together — 'the National Congress to become more socialistic, more proletarian, and organized labour to join the national struggle'.[2]

The nationalist movement, which had been comparatively dormant after the mighty effort of 1921-22, began to rouse itself once more. January 26, 1930 was hailed as Independence Day, and great gatherings all over India stood to take the pledge drafted by Nehru. One sentence of the pledge stated:

> The British Government in India has not only deprived the Indian people of their freedom but has based itself on the exploitation of the masses, and has ruined India economically, politically, culturally, and spiritually.[3]

The pledge set complete independence as the goal, to be pursued by means of non-violent civil disobedience, including non-payment of taxes. Gandhi gave the signal for civil resistance by defying the Salt Act. Thousands of Congress volunteers courted arrest, and the jails were soon overcrowded. The phenomenon of mass *satyagraha* swept the country. Nehru was arrested in April 1930 and sent to Naini Central Prison where, except for eight days of freedom in October, he remained until

[1] *Ibid.*, p. 138.
[2] *Ibid.*, p. 148.
[3] *Ibid.*, p. 388.

January 1931. Nehru had been released in time to be with his father during the last few days of his life. The Delhi Pact, a provisional settlement concluded between Gandhi and Lord Irwin, marked the end of Congress civil disobedience. At the Karachi Congress of 1931 Nehru persuaded the Working Committee to accept a guardedly socialist resolution on fundamental rights and economic policy. The breakdown of new negotiations in London coincided with upheavals in Bengal and new agrarian agitation, and Nehru once more found himself in jail. This term lasted from December 1931 to August 1933.[1]

The 1930s were the most quantitatively productive decade of Nehru's life, from the literary point of view. In this period three important factors combined to enable him to write extensively: the stimulus of newly-acquired socialistic ideas, the intensity of the great events taking shape around him, and the enforced leisure of jail life providing time for study, thought, and writing. *Glimpses of World History* was written in different jails during the period October 1930 to August 1933. Written in the form of letters to his young daughter, this book presented what the title so aptly described — brief insights into history, from the ancient civilizations to the depression of 1929. The political philosophy reflected in *Glimpses of World History* contained most of the elements of his thinking of fifteen years later, although in different proportions.

The basic validity of Western political democracy was presupposed. Perhaps the strongest proof of this fact was Nehru's desire to reveal the democratic values found in ancient Indian traditions.[2]

> But what is very interesting is the freedom of thought and writing in India in the olden days. There was what is known as freedom of conscience. This was not so in Europe till very recent times, and even now there are some disabilities.[3]

Nehru devoted an entire letter to his analysis of 'The Failure of Parliaments'. He found that in parliamentary democracy power had been transferred from the legislative to the executive. A government with a majority in parliament could do

---

[1] *Ibid.*, p. 196.
[2] Jawaharlal Nehru, *Glimpses of World History*, John Day Co., New York, 1942, pp. 111-12, 199, 234, 302.
[3] *Ibid.*, p. 129.

2

almost anything it might decide to do, for turning out a government was a drastic step which 'would result in a lot of trouble
and a general election'.[1] Several other criticisms of the demo-
ratic system which Nehru pointed out were concerned with
this phenomenon of a growing executive domination.

But Nehru's most frequent criticisms of Western political
democracy were socialistic in approach.[2] Political democracy
had produced a superficial and unreal equality by giving
every man one vote. But the poor man's one vote had not
protected him from economic exploitation. 'A vote is of little
use to a hungry man.'[3] Furthermore, parliaments and democratic procedures were always under the control of the capitalist
class. The democratic idea was exploited for undemocratic
purposes. On the international level, Nehru noted the incon-
gruity between British democracy at home and imperialism
abroad, and regarded imperialism as an inevitable consequence
of capitalism. Thus, Nehru concluded that 'real democracy
has had no chance to exist so far, for there is an essential contradiction between the capitalist system and democracy'.[4]

In *Glimpses of World History* Nehru's nationalism was securely
anchored to the Marxist-Leninist interpretation of history. Ten
years earlier his nationalism was chiefly an emotional moral
indignation that India had come under alien rule. In his
statement before the District Magistrate's Court of Allahabad
in 1922, Nehru said that every self-respecting Indian

> has taken a solemn pledge to strive unceasingly for India's freedom,
> so that his countrymen may never again be subjected to the mis-
> eries and humiliations that are the lot of a subject people.[5]

But now imperialism was analyzed in accordance with Marxist
and Leninist theory. Capitalism led 'inevitably' to imperialism,
as raw materials and new markets were required. The inherent
contradictions of the capitalist system were temporarily hidden
only by resort to imperialism.

But much of this wealth and the raising of the standard of living

---

[1] *Ibid.*, p. 934. Nehru quoted Harold Laski's dictum that 'Our government
has become an executive dictatorship tempered by fear of Parliamentary revolt'.
[2] *Ibid.*, pp. 368, 528-32, 553-4, 582, 822-5, 933-5, 955-6.
[3] *Ibid.*, p. 529.
[4] *Ibid.*, p. 935.
[5] *Important Speeches of Jawaharlal Nehru*, ed. J. S. Bright, The Indian Printing
Works, Lahore, 1946, p. 30.

was at the expense of exploited people in Asia, Africa, and other non-industrialized areas. This exploitation and flow of wealth hid for awhile the contradictions of the capitalist system. Even so, the difference between the rich and the poor grew; the distance became greater.[1]

Nevertheless, the British unwittingly became the agents of a great historical process, by which feudal India was being changed into 'the modern kind of industrialized capitalist State'.[2]

Capitalism, and likewise its progeny imperialism, carried within it the seeds of its own destruction. The Indian nationalist movement was part of this inexorable historical process. The British did not understand this process, nor that 'the day of empire is past and the world marches onward relentlessly pushing the British Empire into the "dustbin of history".'[3] In the face of these mighty forces at work, the most one individual could do would be to alter slightly their speed or direction.[4]

Although Marxism provided a rationale for Nehru's nationalism, he did not neglect the internationalism inherent in socialism. Economically, 'the world is essentially international today, although its political structure lags behind and is narrowly national'.[5] The economic problem was essentially an international problem, and the great difficulty was that national rivalries were preventing an international solution. Indeed, the fascists were attempting the intensification of nationalism, which was bound to fail because it was running counter to the international character of the modern world economy. Nehru felt that for a true socialist, nationalism could have no meaning.

If we claim independence today, it is with no desire for isolation. On the contrary, we are perfectly willing to surrender part of that independence, in common with other countries, to a real international order.[6]

One of Nehru's significant contributions to the Indian National

[1] Nehru, *Glimpses of World History*, p. 403.
[2] *Ibid.*, p. 413.
[3] *Loc. cit.*
[4] *Ibid.*, p. 948.
[5] *Ibid.*, p. 873.
[6] Nehru, *Toward Freedom*, p. 267.

Congress was the fostering of what he described as 'the international outlook'.

In *Glimpses of World History* Nehru vigorously propounded the necessity for a socialistic structure of society. Capitalism had many successes to its credit; its organization of big industry had solved the problem of production. But it had failed miserably to meet the problem of distribution. It had increased the wealth enormously, but had kept it in few hands, and the masses had continued to suffer the exploitation of their human resources. Hence the class struggle. The situation demanded a radical cure. Nehru was prepared to see private property abolished completely, for only thus could the way be cleared for the building up of the new society. 'So it is, I think, with imperialism and capitalism. They cannot be improved; the only real improvement is to do away with them altogether.'[1] The struggle between the two rival forces, capitalism and socialism, continued. And there could be no permanent compromise between the two.

During the terms of imprisonment in the early 1930s Nehru read as many books on Marxism as he could lay hands on. The more he read the more deeply he was impressed.

> Russia apart, the theory and philosophy of Marxism lightened up many a dark corner of my mind. History came to have a new meaning for me. The Marxist interpretation threw a flood of light on it, and it became an unfolding drama with some order and purpose, howsoever unconscious, behind it.[2]

He later described Marxism to his daughter in the following manner:

> It is an attempt at reducing human history, past, present and future, to a rigid logical system with something of the inevitability of fate or *kismet* about it.[3]

Regarding the last point Nehru raised the question as to whether life was indeed so logical, and could be reduced to such a rigid system. He quoted with approval Lenin's warning that Marxism should not be considered an inflexible dogma:

> In no sense do we regard the Marxist theory as something complete and unassailable. On the contrary, we are convinced that that

[1] Nehru, *Glimpses of World History*, p. 429.
[2] Nehru, *Toward Freedom*, p. 230.
[3] Nehru, *Glimpses of World History*, p. 544.

theory is only the cornerstone of that science which socialists must advance in all directions if they do not wish to fall behind life.[1]

Nehru was particularly impressed with the great differences in economic background and development between India and Europe, where Marx's theories were formulated.

Nehru pointed out that the rise of Nazism in Germany to a degree confounded orthodox Marxist theory, since the revolutionary elements came not from among the workers, but from the dispossessed lower-middle classes. Nehru's intellectual adherence to Marxism was not disturbed by these developments, as he did not consider it a creed but 'a philosophy of history, a way of looking at history which explains much and makes it hang together, and a method of action to achieve socialism or social equality'.[2] Its fundamental principles had to be adjusted to changing conditions. Nehru's approach to Marxism, despite his obvious enthusiasm for much of it, was to some extent a pragmatic approach. He advised his fifteen-year-old daughter to learn something about these theories because 'they are moving vast masses of men and women today and they may be of help to us in our own country'.[3]

Glimpses of World History reflected Nehru's devotion to science and the scientific method. He suggested several answers to the question, 'What has been this quest of men, and whither does he journey?' But leaving aside the answers provided by religion and philosophy, Nehru stated:

> Science gives a doubting and hesitating reply, for it is of the nature of science not to dogmatize, but to experiment and reason and rely on the mind of man. I need hardly tell you that my preferences are all for science and the methods of science.[4]

This preference for the methods of science was perhaps the only facet of Nehru's thought which remained constant throughout his life, starting with his early college days. A large part of his attraction to communism may be attributed to his belief that 'Marx surveyed past history as a scientist and drew certain conclusions from it'.[5] Nehru wrote that 'it was the essential freedom from dogma and the scientific outlook of

[1] *Ibid.*, p. 548.
[2] *Ibid.*, pp. 920-21.
[3] *Ibid.*, p. 548.
[4] *Ibid.*, p. 173.
[5] *Ibid.*, p. 544.

Marxism that appealed to me'.[1] Nehru attached little significance to his earlier socialistic ideas because they were 'more
humanitarian and utopian than scientific'.[2] Soviet Russia's
Five Year Plan was unique because of the spirit behind it, 'the
spirit of science, an attempt to apply a thought-out scientific
method to the building up of society'.[3]

Considerable space has been devoted to the ideas expressed
in *Glimpses of World History* because this was Nehru's first major
writing, and reflected very clearly his political thinking during
the period 1930-33. Nehru was discharged from Naini Central
Prison in August 1933, and devoted some time to looking
after domestic matters. He met Gandhi, whom he had not
seen for over two years, and prepared a personal campaign 'to
turn people's attention to socialistic doctrines and the world
situation'.[4] Nevertheless, Nehru never identified himself with
the Congress Socialists, organized by Jai Prakash Narain, for
he felt that this was a divisive tendency at a time when nationalist unity was essential.

A few months after his release from prison Nehru accepted
an invitation to address the students of the Banaras Hindu
University. In the course of his speech he launched into an
attack on communalism, and especially the activities of the
Hindu Mahasabha. He later recorded that:

> This was not exactly a premeditated attack, but for a long time
> past my mind had been full of resentment at the increasingly re-
> actionary efforts of the communalists of all groups; and, as I
> warmed up to my subject, some of this resentment came out.[5]

The speech stirred up a controversy of considerable proportions, in the course of which Nehru wrote an article in which
he analyzed both Hindu and Muslim communalism, and attempted to show that both were masks for political and social
reaction. This incident was significant in the development of
his ideas on the secular state.

Gandhi's influence on Nehru in the early 1920s has been
dealt with above. Nehru did not understand Gandhi's talk of sin
and personal salvation, and completely rejected his opposition

[1] Nehru, *Toward Freedom*, p. 230.
[2] *Ibid.*, p. 44.
[3] Nehru, *Glimpses of World History*, p. 857.
[4] Nehru, *Toward Freedom*, p. 257.
[5] *Ibid.*, p. 288.

to industrialization. However he was strongly attracted to Gandhi's ethical principles and *satyagraha*. Ten years later Nehru's socialism had created new areas of tension between himself and Gandhi. Nehru complained that after years of the closest association with Gandhi, he was still not clear in his own mind what Gandhi's objectives were. Gandhi's praise of poverty and the ascetic life, and rejection of much of present-day civilization seemed to distort the social objectives of his movement. Gandhi's approach was completely individualistic. 'He is not out to change society or the social structure; he devotes himself to the eradication of sin from individuals.'[1] What disturbed Nehru most was Gandhi's defence of the *zamindari* system of large landed estates. Gandhi apparently felt that it was a desirable part of rural economy.[2] He stressed the idea of the trusteeship of the possessing classes. The Marxist idea of 'class war' was utterly repugnant to him, as well as the violence associated with communism. Gandhi at times called himself a socialist, but he used the word 'in a sense peculiar to himself which has little or nothing to do with the economic framework of society which usually goes by the name of socialism'.[3] Nehru, on the other hand, held that Gandhi's ideal of the moral individual could never be attained in an environment dominated by the conflict-breeding profit motive.

Nehru once wrote that his father and Gandhi had been the chief personal influences in his life. He posed the question, 'How came we to associate ourselves with Gandhi politically, and to become, in many instances, his devoted followers?' He did not find any completely satisfactory answer, apart from the indefinable element—the strange force of Gandhi's personality. Apparently it was his clear call to action more than anything else which captivated Nehru and others.

Often they did not understand him. But the action that he proposed was something tangible which could be understood and appreciated intellectually. Any action would have been welcome after the long tradition of inaction which our spineless politics had nurtured; brave and effective action with an ethical halo about it had an irresistible appeal, both to the intellect and the emotions.

[1] *Ibid.*, p. 316.
[2] *Ibid.*, p. 295.
[3] *Ibid.*, p. 318.

Step by step he convinced us of the rightness of the action, and we went with him, although we did not accept his philosophy.[1]

Thus, although Nehru considered Gandhi to be ideologically 'sometimes amazingly backward', in action he had proved to be the greatest revolutionary of recent times.[2] Nehru was impatient with the 'parlour socialists' who criticized Gandhi as the 'arch-reactionary'.

But the little fact remains that this 'reactionary' knows India, understands India, almost *is* peasant India, and has shaken up India as no so-called revolutionary has done.[3]

The urge to action has been a constant element of Nehru's temperament and outlook on life.[4] At a crucial point in the nationalist struggle, Gandhi captured this urge to action.

DISILLUSIONMENT: OLD IDEALS AND NEW QUESTIONS

After five and a half months of freedom Nehru was again arrested, in February 1934, and taken to Alipore Jail in Calcutta. From prison he followed the European political upheavals as best he could, and felt depressed by the course of events, especially the rise of fascism in Germany.[5] In April he was further disheartened by the news that Gandhi had withdrawn civil disobedience. As Nehru's health was suffering from the Calcutta air and heat he was transferred to Dehra Dun Jail, and in June began writing his autobiography. His sentence was suspended in September 1935, and Nehru hurried to Germany where his wife was receiving treatment for a critical illness. In January, Nehru received word that he had been elected, for the second time, president of the Indian National Congress. Shortly afterwards Kamala Nehru died, and Nehru returned to India.

Nehru's presidental address delivered to the Indian National Congress in April 1936 was a forceful analysis of the Indian and international political situation from the Marxist-Leninist point of view. He interpreted the post-World War period to show how capitalism and imperialistic rivalries inevitably

[1] *Ibid.*, p. 191.
[2] *Ibid.*, p. 233.
[3] *Ibid.*, p. 258.
[4] *See* Jawaharlal Nehru, *The Discovery of India*, John Day Co., New York, 1946, Chap. I, Part iv, entitled 'Time in Prison: the Urge to Action'.
[5] Nehru, *Toward Freedom*, pp. 306-7.

continued to breed conflict. The world had never settled down after the war, for new economic and political conditions were such that the existing structure could not cope with them. A great depression overwhelmed the world, and only in the Soviet Union was progress being made, 'although often at terrible cost'.[1] Capitalism, facing unprecedented difficulties,

> took to fascism with all its brutal suppression of what Western civilization had apparently stood for; it became, even in some of its homelands, what its imperialist counterpart had long been in the subject colonial countries.[2]

Fascism and imperialism were thus two faces of decaying capitalism. Nehru urged Congressmen to try to develop 'the historic sense', so that they could understand their national problem as 'but a part of the world problem of capitalist imperialism'.[3]

Turning more directly to the Indian nationalist movement, Nehru showed Lenin's influence on his thinking when he stated that

> paradoxically, it is only from the middle-class intellectuals that revolutionary leadership comes, and we in India know that our bravest leaders and our stoutest comrades have come from the ranks of the middle classes.[4]

This must 'inevitably' be the case; nevertheless, the Congress should look increasingly to the masses and draw strength from them.

Although Nehru's election to the presidency was in no way regarded as an endorsement of socialism by the Congress, still he felt that it indicated a growing interest in these ideas which he personally embraced with no little conviction.

> I am convinced that the only key to the solution of the world's problems and of India's problems lies in socialism, and, when I use this word, I do so not in a vague humanitarian way but in the scientific economic sense. Socialism is, however, something even more than an economic doctrine; it is a philosophy of life, and as such also it appeals to me.[5]

Nehru pointed to the new socialist civilization of Soviet

[1] *Ibid.*, p. 392. The speech is included in this book as Appendix B.
[2] *Ibid.*, p. 393.
[3] *Ibid.*, p. 400.
[4] *Ibid.*, p. 397.
[5] *Ibid.*, p. 400.

Russia. Despite many developments there which had pained him greatly, Nehru still looked upon 'that great and fascinating unfolding of a new order and a new civilization as the most promising feature of our dismal age'.[1] Nehru epitomised his glowing faith in socialism in the following words: 'Socialism is thus for me not merely an economic doctrine which I favour; it is a vital creed which I hold with all my head and heart'.[2] The year 1936 and thereabout may be regarded as the period marking the peak of Nehru's intellectual adherence and emotional attachment to socialism.

Nehru found it difficult to work smoothly with many of his own colleagues, and tensions developed within the Congress executive. Many disliked the socialistic trend of Nehru's leadership.[3] He was about to resign when news of Franco's revolt in Spain reached him, and affected him greatly. Nehru saw in this crisis the beginning of a European or even world conflict, and felt that unity in the Congress ranks was essential.

> The reaction of the Spanish War on me indicates how, in my mind, the problem of India was tied up with other world problems. More and more I came to think that these separate problems, political or economic, in China, Abyssinia, Spain, Central Europe, India, or elsewhere, were facets of one and the same world problem.[4]

Despite continued tensions between the more moderate and the more left-wing sections of the Congress, Nehru was re-elected president, his third term in all.

The new constitution proposed in the Government of India Act of 1935 was rejected on principle by the National Congress. Nevertheless, in 1937 the Congress decided to contest the elections held under the constitution. Although Nehru was not a candidate, he toured all over India in the election campaign, travelling about fifty-thousand miles in four months. His impressions of that extensive tour gripped him profoundly — 'For me it was a voyage of discovery of India and her people'— and caused him later, in the quiet of Ahmadnagar Fort prison, to write *The Discovery of India*.[5]

---

[1] *Ibid.*, p. 401.
[2] *Loc. cit.*
[3] Nehru, *Toward Freedom*, p. 358. Jawaharlal Nehru, *The Unity of India: Collected Writings 1937-40*, John Day Co., New York, 1948, pp. 94-102.
[4] Nehru, *Toward Freedom*, pp. 358-9.
[5] *Ibid.*, p. 360.

In 1938 Nehru flew to Spain to see the civil war at close quarters. He visited England, then Czechoslovakia, and as the conflict spread, Nehru was disappointed by 'the utter collapse, in the moment of crisis, of all the so-called advanced people and groups'.[1] He later wrote:

> I was affected more than others by the development of events in Europe and the Far East. Munich was a shock hard to bear, and the tragedy of Spain became a personal sorrow to me. As these years of horror succeeded one another, the sense of impending catastrophe overwhelmed me, and my faith in a bright future for the world became dim.[2]

Returning to India, Nehru was disheartened by the growing communal spirit, and especially the activities of the Muslim League. Under M. A. Jinnah's leadership the League in 1940 finally demanded the partition of India and the creation of a separate Muslim state.

Nehru was discouraged by the trend of Congress politics and openly repudiated certain decisions which, in his opinion, Gandhi had arbitrarily imposed on the Congress. In 1939 he wrote:

> More and more the choice before many of us becomes difficult, and this is no question of Right or Left or even of political decision. The choice is of unthinking acceptance of decisions which sometimes contradict one another and have no logical sequence, or opposition, or inaction. . . . No great movement can be carried on on this basis; certainly not a democratic movement.[3]

Nehru devoted considerable attention to the activities of the All-India States' Peoples' Conference, and to the National Planning Committee formed under Congress auspices. The latter work served to introduce Nehru to the practical problems involved in national planning, although the recommendations of the Committee could only be put into effect after independence.

Indicative of his intellectual interests is the list of books which Nehru took with him on a brief vacation in the Himalayas in 1939. Included were Aldous Huxley's *Ends and Means*, Bertrand Russell's *Which Way to Peace*, John Dewey's *The*

---

[1] *Ibid.*, p. 363.
[2] *Ibid.*, p. 356.
[3] *Ibid.*, p. 366.

Quest for Certainty, and Levy's *Philosophy for a Modern Man*.[1] He made a brief visit to China in August 1939 and returned hurriedly after the outbreak of World War II. The British Government refused to clarify its war aims in terms of Indian independence, and the Congress prepared once more for civil disobedience.

The entire period from the death of Nehru's wife in 1936 through the early years of World War II was, for Nehru, one of severe disillusionment. His idealism was shocked by the horrors of the war, and his optimism and confidence in a bright future for the world became clouded. Internal conflicts within the Congress and disappointment with Gandhi's course of action heightened his distress. Soviet Russia's role in the game of power politics came as an even greater shock to him.

> As the war progressed, new problems arose or the old problems took new shape, and the old alignments seemed to change, the old standards to fade away. There were many shocks, and adjustment was difficult. The Russo-German Pact, the Soviet's invasion of Finland, the friendly approach of Russia toward Japan. Were there any principles, or any standards of conduct in the world, or was it all sheer opportunism?[2]

Nehru had never been blind to the realities of the Russian 'dictatorship of the proletariat', as his small book *Soviet Russia* showed. In *Glimpses of World History* he pointed out that individual freedom was severely curtailed in Russia and that violence was often resorted to on a large scale.[3]

Whatever doubts might have arisen regarding Russia's internal conditions, her foreign policy had been consistent, straightforward, and peaceful. Nehru could assert without any qualification his profound conviction that: 'Year after year this policy was based on peace, collective security and the aiding and encouragement of those who resisted aggression'.[4] But the events of 1939-40 were difficult to explain, and the articles written by Nehru in this period reflected his inner anxiety, perplexity and disillusionment.[5] He cautioned his

---

[1] John Gunther, *Inside Asia*, Harper and Brothers, New York, 1939, p. 439.
[2] Nehru, *Toward Freedom*, p. 370.
[3] Nehru, *Glimpses of World History*, pp. 822, 857.
[4] Jawaharlal Nehru, *China, Spain and the War*, Kitabistan, Allahabad, 1940, pp. 251-2.
[5] *Ibid.*, p. 242.

readers not to be deceived by the one-sided news and pro-
paganda about Russia emanating from the capitalist countries.
He described Russia's policies as 'paying back the imperialist
Powers in their own coin'.[1] He explained the invasion of
Finland as Russia's move to forestall an anti-Soviet front inva-
sion of Russia.[2]

In these articles Nehru's mind seemed to swing like a pendu-
lum between alternate justification, and sad and reluctant
condemnation of Russia's *real politik*. Although the above ex-
planations were offered, still Nehru had to conclude that

> Soviet Russia, their symbol of hope and fulfilment, has descended
> from the pedestal on which her ardent champions had placed her,
> and bartered away her moral prestige and the friendship of so
> many of her friends for seeming political advantage.[3]

Referring to the invasion of Finland, Nehru wrote that Russia

> has paid heavily for this vital error, and paid in a coin which
> cannot be counted, for it is made up of the wishes and ideals of
> innumerable human beings.[4]

Nehru stated that Russia had injured the cause of socialism
by associating aggression with it. He reminded his readers that
there was no necessary connection between the Soviet government and socialism. Nevertheless, there could be little doubt
that the war years had deeply affected Nehru's devotion to
socialism as well as his admiration of Soviet Russia. The rather
doctrinaire socialism of his 1936 Lucknow Congress address
started to give way. In his article of January 1940, 'What of
Russia Now?', Nehru concluded on this note of uncertainty:

> We have to remember yet again that in this revolutionary age of
> transition and change, when all our old values are upset and we
> seek new standards, we must retain our integrity of mind and
> purpose . . .[5]

REVALUATION: HUMANISM AND THE SCIENTIFIC SPIRIT

Congress negotiations with the British Government again
broke down in 1940, the Viceroy's proposal having fallen far
short of the demand for national independence. Individual

[1] *Ibid.*, p. 244.
[2] *Ibid.*, pp. 245-6.
[3] *Ibid.*, p. 250.
[4] *Ibid.*, p. 253.
[5] *Ibid.*, p. 257.

civil disobedience was declared, and Gandhi was appointed
as leader of the movement. Nehru was arrested in October
1940 and remained in Dehra Dun Jail until December 1941,
spending most of his time in reading and gardening. Sir Stafford
Cripps came from England with new proposals for constitutional changes, and once more the negotiations ended abruptly
in failure. In August 1942 the All-India Congress Committee
debated in public and passed the 'Quit India Resolution', and
a few days later Nehru was in Ahmadnagar Fort Prison. This
term of almost three years lasted until June 1945. During the
period April-September 1944 Nehru produced what many consider his best writing, *The Discovery of India*.

In this book Nehru surveyed 'the panorama of India's past'
and found new inspiration in the continuity of her culture and
traditions throughout five thousand years of history. Of his
approach to India Nehru commented: 'To some extent I came
to her via the West and looked at her as a friendly Westerner
might have done.'[1] He indeed found in Indian thought and
traditions much that attracted him. But what he appreciated
most in India's past were ideas and attitudes which seemed to
coalesce with his own philosophy, which had already been
formed essentially from Western sources.

The first two chapters of *The Discovery of India*, however, were
mainly devoted to autobiographical material, and in the section on 'Life's Philosophy' Nehru sought to analyze his own
philosophy of life. Referring to the period leading up to World
War II he admitted that his spiritual and philosophical
foundations had been weakened.

> What was my philosophy of life? I did not know. Some years
> earlier I would not have been so hesitant. There was a definiteness
> about my thinking and objectives then which has faded away
> since. The events of the past few years in India, China, Europe,
> and all over the world have been confusing, upsetting and dis-
> tressing, and the future has become vague and shadowy and has
> lost that clearness of outline which it once possessed in my mind.[2]

Along with this inner perplexity Nehru had experienced a
growing distaste for politics, and 'gradually my whole attitude
to life seemed to undergo a transformation'.

[1] Nehru, *The Discovery of India*, p. 38.
[2] *Ibid.*, p. 13.

The ideals and objectives of yesterday were still the ideals of today but they had lost some of their lustre, and even as one seemed to go toward them they lost the shining beauty which had warmed the heart and vitalized the body.[1]

Nehru had hitherto taken a basically optimistic attitude toward human nature, but he now despaired of the possibility of changing it and raising man 'above that creature of lust and violence and deceit that he now was'.[2]

Nehru by 1944 seemed to approach the subject of religion in a more sympathetic manner than was evidenced in his earlier writings. He still disliked the superstitious practices and dogmas often associated with religion, but nevertheless appreciated the fact that it had given a set of moral and ethical values to human life. Furthermore, he could commit himself personally to the observation that:

Life does not consist entirely of what we see and hear and feel, the visible world which is undergoing change in time and space. It is continually touching an invisible world of other, and possibly more stable or equally changeable elements, and no thinking person can ignore this invisible world.[3]

Nehru claimed to have no interest whatsoever in the question of a future life, and the idea of a personal God was completely foreign to his way of thinking. His closest approximation to a religious feeling was a sense of awe when he contemplated the mysteries of the universe. Nevertheless as to the question of what the mysterious was Nehru could only say, 'I do not know'.[4] In an earlier book he had recorded his attraction to the traditional Chinese outlook which was 'fundamentally ethical and yet irreligious or tinged with religious scepticism'.[5]

Although in *The Discovery of India* Nehru recorded his previous loss of faith in human nature, apparently he had regained it by 1944, and his idealism reasserted itself in the following sentence:

How amazing is this spirit of man! In spite of innumerable failings, man, throughout the ages, has sacrificed his life and all he held dear for an ideal, for truth, for faith, for country and honour. That

[1] *Loc. cit.*
[2] *Loc. cit.*
[3] *Ibid.*, p. 14.
[4] *Ibid.*, p. 16.
[5] Nehru, *Toward Freedom*, p. 242.

ideal may change, but that capacity for self-sacrifice continues, and because of that, much may be forgiven to man, and it is impossible to lose hope for him.[1]

Nehru sensed the essential nobility of man seeking to master the mighty forces of nature, but he now recognized that there was also something of the devil in man.

Nehru's humanist credo was presented in one terse question: 'God we may deny, but what hope is there for us if we deny Man and thus reduce everything to futility?'[2] The meaning of life is to be found in the 'exciting adventure of Man', the struggle to attain ideals which continue to grow just as Man continues to grow.[3] The humanism of Rabindranath Tagore influenced Nehru considerably. Nehru wrote: 'Tagore was the great humanist of India.'[4] More than any other Indian thinker, Tagore had helped to harmonize the ideals of India and the West. Nehru quoted from Tagore's deathbed message, in which he expressed his profound distress over a crumbling Western civilization (Tagore died in 1941), but asserted, 'And yet I shall not commit the grievous sin of losing faith in Man'.[5]

In 'Life's Philosophy' Nehru acknowledged the great effect on his thinking produced by the study of Marx and Lenin.

Much in the Marxist philosophical outlook I could accept without difficulty; its monism and nonduality of mind and matter, the dynamics of matter and the dialectic of continuous change by evolution as well as leap, through action and interaction, cause and effect, thesis, antithesis, and synthesis.[6]

Nehru recognized the difficulty of reconciling dialectical materialism with the idealism in other areas of his thinking, especially with his ideas regarding the ethical approach to life. As he put it, 'there was an odd mixture in my mind which I could not rationally explain or resolve'.[7] While Nehru had accepted the basic tenets of socialism, he rejected the approach of dogmatic adherence to it, because life is 'too illogical to be confined within the four corners of a fixed doctrine'.[8]

[1] Nehru, *The Discovery of India*, p. 21.
[2] *Ibid.*, p. 477.
[3] *Ibid.*, p. 521.
[4] *Ibid.*, p. 342.
[5] *Ibid.*, p. 477.
[6] *Ibid.*, p. 17.
[7] *Ibid.*, p. 18.
[8] *Ibid.*, p. 19.

In Nehru's statement of his life philosophy as of 1944, he defined the sphere of philosophy in terms of human problems.

....We must beware of losing ourselves in a sea of speculation unconnected with the day-to-day problems of life and the needs of men and women. A living philosophy must answer the problems of today.[1]

The most important criterion of a philosophy was not coherence or comprehensiveness, but workability. It must meet man's needs. And by what method should the day-to-day problems of life be tackled, and by what approach should their solutions be sought? 'In the solution of these problems the way of observation and precise knowledge and deliberate reasoning, according to the method of science, must be followed.'[2] The key to the methodology was 'precise objective knowledge tested by reason and even more so by experiment and practice'.[3] It was essentially the experimental method which would lead both to the solution of individual problems and to the formulation of a valid philosophy of life.

Pragmatism thus emerged as a strong current in the stream of Nehru's personal philosophy. In the last chapter of *The Discovery of India* Nehru revealed much of his own mind when he wrote,

The modern mind, that is to say the better type of the modern mind, is practical and pragmatic, ethical and social, altruistic and humanitarian.[4]

It would have been difficult to find six words which could have more accurately described Nehru's approach to life. He further stated:

We have therefore to function in line with the highest ideals of the age we live in, though we may add to them or seek to mould them in accordance with our national genius. Those ideals may be classed under two heads; humanism and the scientific spirit.[5]

Nehru noted a growing synthesis between the two, resulting in a kind of scientific humanism.

[1] *Loc. cit.*
[2] *Loc. cit.*
[3] *Loc. cit.*
[4] *Ibid.*, p. 570.
[5] *Ibid.*, p. 571.

3

ACHIEVEMENT: INDEPENDENCE AND AFTER

Nehru was released from prison in June 1945, and events moved swiftly in the direction of Indian independence. In February 1946 a Cabinet Mission was sent to India by the new British Labour Government to draw up a plan of self-government for the country. The plan which was proposed engendered further controversy between the Indian National Congress and the Muslim League. In August 1946 Nehru, in his capacity as Congress President, was asked by Lord Wavell, the Viceroy, to form a government at the centre. This was done and Nehru headed the Interim Government until the time of partition. The Labour Government sent out Lord Mountbatten as the new Governor-General. In rapid succession partition was agreed upon, the Indian Independence Act was passed, and on August 15, 1947, independence and partition were effected.

The immediate post-independence period was one of heavy responsibility for Nehru, who continued to head the Cabinet of the new India after the partition. Partition brought in its wake communal upheavals of unprecedented magnitude in the Punjab, and later in Bengal. Millions of people migrated across the new borders in both directions, creating a refugee problem of great proportions. Two and a half months after the partition a full scale war broke out between India and Pakistan in the disputed state of Kashmir. Three months later Gandhi was assassinated by a Hindu communal fanatic.

Despite the pressure of these problems, work on the new Constitution of India was continued in the Constituent Assembly, which had been formed in 1946. Nehru assumed an important role in the early stages of this work by moving the Objectives Resolution which set forth the basic aims of the Constituent Assembly in drafting the Constitution.[1] He served as chairman of the Union Constitution Committee, which was charged with reporting on the principles to be embodied in the Union Constitution. The report of this Committee, submitted on July 4, 1947, shaped the general structure and many of the provisions incorporated in the finalized form of the Constitution. Nehru's participation in the later work of the Constituent Assembly was necessarily limited due to the

[1] Jawaharlal Nehru, *Independence and After: Collection of Speeches, 1946-1949*, John Day Co., New York, 1950, p. 344.

weighty responsibilities of premiership in that period. A highly significant decision in which Nehru took the lead was that providing for India's continued membership in the Common-wealth of Nations.[1] The final draft of the Constitution was approved by the Constituent Assembly in November 1949, and became effective on January 26, 1950. The first elections under the new Constitution were held in 1951-52, the largest demo-cratic elections ever held in any country, in which an electorate of 106 million people participated. The elections confirmed the Congress Government and Nehru's leadership.

A cease-fire in Kashmir was arranged through the good offices of a United Nations Commission and became effective in January 1949. Although no final solution of the Kashmir question was reached, the tension was eased, and Nehru turned his attention increasingly to the wider international problems connected with the 'cold war'. He steadfastly refused to align India with either the Soviet or the Western bloc. Nehru depre-cated charges that India's foreign policy was one of oppor-tunistic neutrality. He described it rather as a positive policy seeking to bring about world peace, and this claim has been validated, in the opinion of many, by India's significant role in the termination of the Korean and Indo-China conflicts.

Nehru's stature as an international statesman has risen con-siderably from 1949 to the present. He has taken the lead in seek-ing the co-operation of Asian and African countries in working toward common goals, such as the elimination of imperialism and racial inequality, and economic advancement.[2]

What have been the most significant developments in Nehru's political thinking from 1947 to 1957? Obviously, the coming of independence and the responsibility of high public office almost completely reversed the circumstances in which Nehru's political philosophy had developed. For over thirty years he had been a nationalist 'agitator'; he now became Prime Minister. This new situation could not but affect his political ideas.

One of the major developments has been a much deeper probing of the meaning, scope, difficulties, and validity of the

[1] *Ibid.*, p. 265.
[2] *See* Werner Levi, *Free India in Asia*, University of Minnesota Press, Minnea-polis, 1952.

democratic structure of the state. Up to 1947 Nehru more or less presupposed democracy as the base of his political thinking. As he remarked in his autobiography,

> My roots are still perhaps partly in the nineteenth century, and I have been too much influenced by the humanist liberal tradition to get out of it completely.[1]

He did comparatively little thinking on the subject. Where democracy is mentioned in his pre-1947 writings it is usually in connection with one of the two dominant themes—nationalism and socialism. In the case of the former, his ideas on fundamental rights and a constituent assembly, for example, were used as focal points for demanding national independence. In the case of the latter, the unreality of political democracy apart from economic and social democracy was his usual emphasis. But as the goal of independence was approached Nehru's attention was turned to the drafting of the Indian Constitution. Later, in parliamentary debates, he has had to come to grips with legislation directly impinging on the broader problems of democracy.

A second major development in Nehru's post-independence political thinking has been the continued modification of his socialism. This subject is dealt with in more detail in the chapters on economic democracy. Only the broad trends are outlined here. From the point of view of practical politics, securing the co-operation of the diverse elements within the Congress Party would necessitate certain modifications of his socialism in policy if not in personal philosophy. But as has been pointed out, the modification of Nehru's socialism was a process which began ten years before independence.[2] The process might be described as follows. Nehru's attachment to science and the scientific method was formed early in life, and has remained the one constant factor in his life philosophy up to the present time. The great attraction of socialism was that Nehru saw in it the scientific approach to economic and social problems.[3] Events leading up through World War II had the effect of shaking up many of his former values and ideas, socialism among them. Nevertheless he held on to his faith in

---

[1] Nehru, *Toward Freedom*, p. 348.
[2] *Supra*, pp. 30-1.
[3] *Supra*, pp. 23-4.

science, and gradually the pragmatism which is a possible corollary of the experimental method asserted itself in Nehru's thinking about economics.

Nehru's present approach may be summarized as follows: (1) the foremost objective is to raise the standard of living of India's masses; (2) production is the first problem since you cannot distribute what you have not produced; (3) large scale nationalization of the existing means of production would not necessarily increase production, and would expend the State's limited financial resources in the payment of compensation, and thus divert it from building up new and productive State industries; (4) any measures consistent with democratic procedure may be utilized to attain the objective. Nehru wrote in 1952, 'The only test of any system that we apply is that it gives us the desired results.'[1] (5) an economic structure providing for both a private sector, in which a regulated form of free enterprise would operate, and an expanding public sector, with State-owned and controlled industry, promises to give India the desired results.

In the preceding pages an effort has been made to trace chronologically the main currents of Nehru's political thinking, and to indicate the most significant events, ideas and people that have influenced his thinking. As one rapidly surveys his life, five years stand out as marking significant events or trends which helped to mould Nehru's philosophy. In 1905 he went to England for his education. Seven of the most formative years of his life were spent in the West, and Nehru's basic outlook on life was deeply influenced by this experience. In 1920 Nehru had an experience with the peasants which greatly altered his 'bourgeois' outlook, and made him aware of the oppressed masses of India. Gandhi's influence on him was also great in this period, and deepened this concern for the peasantry.

In 1926-27 Nehru visited Europe and for the first time came into fairly intimate contact with socialists and communists, and returned to India a convinced socialist. 1936 marked Nehru's presidential address to the Lucknow Congress, and this date may be taken rather arbitrarily to indicate the peak

[1] Jawaharlal Nehru, *Report to the All-India Congress Committee*, All-India Congress Committee, New Delhi, 1951, p. 10.

of his adherence to a somewhat doctrinaire socialism, which
declined under the pressures of the following five years. In 1947
independence was attained, and this marked the fulfilment
of one great life goal for Nehru. It also marked the beginning
of official responsibility in the new India, and the challenge
to transform political ideals into political realities.

III

THE MEANING OF DEMOCRACY

My own feeling is that the whole system of democracy is coming up against several inherent difficulties. Perhaps my honourable friends opposite—some of them, at any rate—will term these 'inner contradictions'. Perhaps, they really are so.

Speech in Parliament, 1952.

CHAPTER III

THE MEANING OF DEMOCRACY

IN probing for the sources of Nehru's democratic thought, one must resist the temptation to be more specific than the facts warrant. One could take the speeches and writings of almost any twentieth-century democratic politician, and trace the ideas contained therein back to theorists whose names he might vaguely recall, but whose books he had never read. His ideas would probably be a combination of Locke, Rousseau, Montesquieu, Bentham, J. S. Mill, etc., and not without traces of Marx. That is to say, ideas which were once the distinctive theories of individual philosophers and their conscious followers, have filtered down to become the common property of almost all. Therefore, to say simply that the hypothetical politician referred to above had been influenced by Rousseau would be somewhat misleading.

This is to some extent the problem encountered in discussing the sources of Nehru's ideas. He did not 'discover' Western political democracy as he did the socialism of Karl Marx. He grew up in an intellectual environment which assumed it. His father, steeped in the principles of British constitutional law, presupposed parliamentary democracy as the natural structure of government. As a law student in England, Nehru's thinking developed within the same framework of generally accepted ideas.

In his books Nehru quotes Montesquieu's *Esprit des Lois*, Rousseau's *Du Contrat Social* ('Man is born free, but is everywhere in chains'), and John Stuart Mill's *On Liberty*, all of which apparently made a considerable impression on his mind. But it is probable that Nehru's reading of these and other political philosophers did little more than confirm, clarify, and intensify ideas which he already had. He wrote in 1935: 'My roots are still perhaps partly in the nineteenth century, and I have been too much influenced by the humanist liberal tradition to get out of it completely.' Nehru's democratic thought is more the product of this broad *tradition*, the humanist liberal tradition, than of specific sources.

Precisely what does Nehru mean when he uses the word *democracy*? It is obvious that the content of the word has varied at different stages of his life. In his early years in the struggle for independence, the ideal of democracy was very closely related to the goal of self-rule for India. Democracy meant freedom from foreign rule and a truly representative government. Nehru's later socialist ideas strongly altered his understanding of democracy. But even at present, Nehru uses the word in several different, although related, ways. The broad and inclusive meanings which he sometimes attaches to the word are indicated by the following statement.

> I would say that democracy is not only political, not only economic but something of the mind, as everything is ultimately something of the mind. It involves equality of opportunity to all people, as far as possible, in the political and economic domain. It involves the freedom of the individual to grow and to make the best of his capacities and ability. It involves a certain tolerance of others and even of others' opinions when they differ from yours. It involves a certain inquisitive search for truth—and for, let us say, the right thing. That is, it is a dynamic, not a static, thing, and as it changes it may be that its domain will become wider and wider. Ultimately, it is a mental approach applied to our political and economic problems.[1]

Four important definitions emerge from a careful study of Nehru's usage of the word. Three of them may be found in the statement quoted above.

These definitions are in reality different approaches or emphases in Nehru's thinking about democracy, and there is naturally a certain overlapping. The four definitions may be classified as follows: (1) Democracy defined in terms of the freedom in which human values can be realized; (2) Democracy defined in terms of certain governmental institutions and procedures; (3) Democracy defined in terms of a structure of society in which economic and social equality will gradually be attained; (4) Democracy defined in terms of a certain attitude and approach to problems on the part of the individual and society. The present chapter is devoted to an exposition of these four definitions of democracy.

---

[1] Cousins, *Talks with Nehru*, pp. 18-19.

DEMOCRACY AS INDIVIDUAL FREEDOM

According to Nehru, the democratic state is one in which there is freedom for the realization of human values and the creative development of the individual. Nehru has expressed great concern for the fate of the individual in the twentieth century. The purpose of a democratic society is 'to provide the individual with the conditions of creative development'.[1] Yet these essential conditions are shrinking in the modern world. Nehru was perturbed by a 'de-individualization and brutalization of individual man'.

> More and more the individual is giving way to the crowd. When he is by himself, he can be approached and he is responsive to reason. You can appeal to the good that is inherent in him; he has a sense of responsibility. His conscience, if not always in absolute control, is at least a factor in his decisions and actions. But then he is attracted to the crowd and strange things begin to happen. The crowd seldom places the reins on itself that the individual often feels compelled to do. The crowd dominates the individual but lacks a conscience of its own. Almost everywhere today the individual is giving himself over to the crowd or is being seized by it. The crowd is a brute. The crowd terrifies me.[2]

Nehru attributed this process of the coarsening and vulgarization of the individual to the succession of wars and violence. It is 'the mentality that is bred by war'.[3] He asserted in one speech in Parliament that if this process were to continue, he doubted 'whether for many sensitive persons life will offer very much of value at all'.[4]

Nevertheless, the democratic state still represents a structure of society in which freedom is cherished, and in which human values can best be realized. In *Glimpses of World History* Nehru made several references to the freedom of thought, writing, and conscience which had existed in India for centuries.[5] On December 13, 1946 Nehru moved the Objectives Resolution

[1] *Ibid.*, p. 6.

[2] *Loc. cit.* Compare José Ortega y Gasset, *The Revolt of the Masses*, New American Library of World Literature, Inc., New York, 1950. 'The mass crushes beneath it everything that is different, everything that is excellent, individual, qualified and select' (p. 12). 'The mass-man is simply without morality, which is always, in essence, a sentiment of submission to something, a consciousness of service and obligation' (p. 140).

[3] *Parliamentary Debates, 1950*, Vol. VI, Part II, col. 1382.

[4] *Loc. cit.*

[5] Nehru, *Glimpses of World History*, p. 129.

in which the Constituent Assembly declared its intention of drawing up a Constitution guaranteeing and securing 'to all the people of India .... freedom of thought, expression, belief, faith, worship, vocation, association and action'.[1] Independent India had chosen democracy and individual freedom, because it offered the highest dividends.

When I say highest dividends, I do not mean merely material dividends although they are important but cultural and spiritual dividends also. Intellectual freedom is an important factor, certainly; but the future will show its worth. We have deliberately chosen a democratic setup and we feel that it is good for our people and for our country in the ultimate analysis.[2]

India's long tradition of intellectual freedom, as well as Western democratic thought, had found its expression in the Constitution of free India.

Nehru wrote in 1933 that in a democracy, the government is after all a means to an end, namely, the 'good life'. While definitions of the 'good life' might differ, most people would agree that freedom is essential to it.

National freedom so far as the nation is concerned, personal freedom so far as the individual is concerned. For every restriction and inhibition stops growth and development, and produces, apart from economic disorders, complexes and perversions in the nation and individual. So freedom is necessary.[3]

It is only in the democratic framework that these human values can be obtained, according to Nehru. The authoritarian systems do not permit the growth and development of the individual. Fascism offered man fulfilment, not through his personality or individual self, but through complete and blind obedience to the state.[4] 'Communism,' Nehru asserted, 'for all its triumphs in many fields, crushes the free spirit of man.'[5] Referring to the absence of freedom of speech in the U.S.S.R., Nehru declared,

India cannot follow such a policy. It ultimately hampers the

[1] Nehru, *Independence and After*, p. 344.
[2] Speech in the House of the People, February 18, 1953. *Jawaharlal Nehru's Speeches, 1949-53*, Ministry of Information and Broadcasting, Government of India, Calcutta, 1954, p. 252.
[3] Jawaharlal Nehru, *Recent Essays and Writings*, Kitabistan, Allahabad, 1934, p. 44.
[4] Nehru, *Glimpses of World History*, p. 825.
[5] *Presidential Address, 57th session, Indian National Congress*, October 18, 1951.

progress of the nation by restricting the creative faculties of the common man.[1]

'Nothing', Nehru held, 'can be worse for the world, I think, than a deprivation of human freedom of the individual.'[2] If the individual's growth and creative abilities are suppressed, the group and the nation will ultimately suffer.

Nehru described the rise of eighteenth-century liberalism as essentially a reaction against the autocracy and absolutism of that period.[3] This reaction led to an excessive emphasis on the rights of individuals, as reflected in the French Declaration of the Rights of Man. From his socialist position, Nehru never doubted the basic validity of the emphasis on human freedom. Rather, his criticisms were directed at the over-simplification of the problem ('In a complex society it is not an easy matter to separate individuals and give them perfect freedom')[4] and at the failure to take into account man's economic needs ('happiness did not come by merely making it a fundamental right').[5] The doctrine of individual freedom was essential, but it had been perverted by the failure to give it a social and economic dimension.

The modern democratic state is frequently confronted with the problem of defining the relationship between individual freedom and order in society.[6] Nehru clearly described the inevitability of this problem when he declared:

> Unless the State is perfect and every individual is perfect, there is always some conflict between the freedom of the individual and the security of the State.[7]

The question was by no means a merely academic one for Nehru and his government. Referring to the terrible communal violence in Delhi and the Punjab in 1947, which was in part incited by irresponsible individuals and groups, Nehru

[1] Speech at Farrukhabad. *The Hindu*, December 11, 1949, p. 8.

[2] Speech in San Francisco, November 1, 1949. Jawaharlal Nehru, *Visit to America*, John Day Co., New York, 1950, p. 136.

[3] Nehru, *Glimpses of World History*, p. 368.

[4] *Ibid.*, p. 529.

[5] *Ibid.*, p. 532.

[6] This problem is dealt with in Chapter IV, 'Fundamental Rights in the Indian Crucible', where Nehru's ideas on the rights of personal liberty and freedom of the press are discussed.

[7] Speech in the House of the People, August 2, 1952. *Jawaharlal Nehru's Speeches, 1949-53*, p. 583.

deprecated the idea that such action must be tolerated in order not to violate the abstract principle of freedom of speech.

> If, in the name of democracy, you want people to be incited to do wrong and the structure of a democratic state we have built up undermined, you are welcome to it. Only it is not my conception of democracy.[1]

No simple formula could be given as to where to draw the line between the freedom of the individual and the security and order of the state. It all depended on the circumstances of the particular case. However, Nehru felt that in general 'in times of war the demarcation should be in favour of the State and in peace it should be to the advantage of the individual'.[2]

Another problem which confronts the modern democratic state is that of preserving individual freedom in the face of the universal trend toward centralization.

> The deep problem of today, to put it in this way, is this: You cannot escape centralized authority, whether it is of the state, whether it is of the big corporation, whether it is of the trade union, or whether it is of any group. They all go on being centralized authorities. Now all centralization is a slight encroachment on the freedom of the individual. We want to preserve the freedom of the individual, and at the same time we cannot escape centralization in modern society. How to balance the two?[3]

Writing on 'The Failure of Parliaments', Nehru noted the constant and decided trend in the British Parliament for more and more power to become concentrated in the Cabinet, and correspondingly removed from the House of Commons. At the present time the individual members have very little say in the decisions which are reached. As the executive branch continues to arrogate to itself increasing powers, 'Parliament thus is getting more and more out of touch with important activities of the State'.[4]

The process of centralization has not ended with the executive members of government who are responsible to the people through elections. The system of administration in the modern state is so complex and technical that, inevitably, certain decisions must be left to the judgment of the experts. A

[1] *Ibid.*, p. 582.
[2] *Ibid.*, p. 583.
[3] Cousins, *Talks with Nehru*, pp. 23-4.
[4] Nehru, *Glimpses of World History*, p. 934.

democratically elected parliament finds it almost impossible to deal with these questions.

> So the civil servants or the technical establishment became progressively more and more independent because nobody could understand or control them.[1]

Nehru considered that 'the whole democratic structure of government is rather imperilled by this development'.[2]

What will happen to individual freedom if the present trend toward centralization of authority continues, not only in fascist or communist states, but, as has been pointed out above, in the democratic states as well? Nehru considers increased centralization as not only inevitable in the larger scheme of modern world conditions, but desirable and necessary in order to bring about the economic development of India. It is only through a 'democratically planned collectivism' that the country can scientifically apply all of its resources to solve the great economic problems confronting it.[3] Nehru regarded India's experiments in national planning as an attempt to solve one of the central problems of modern times: 'how to maintain individual freedom and initiative and yet have centralized social control and planning of the economic life of the people'.[4] Thus, although beset by many problems, individual freedom is absolutely essential to the modern democratic state, and in Nehru's view democracy would cease to exist without a wide area of freedom for the realization of human values.

DEMOCRACY AS REPRESENTATIVE GOVERNMENT

Democracy, according to Nehru's thought, must be defined also in terms of representative institutions — government which is responsible ultimately to the people. Some of the elements included in this concept of democracy are popular sovereignty through elected representatives, majority rule, and responsible political parties and leaders.

Popular sovereignty through elected representatives. Nehru has pointed out that ideas of popular sovereignty are by no means foreign to Indian traditions. Throughout Sanskrit literature, and as far back as the *Arthashastra*, it is repeatedly emphasized

[1] India, *Constituent Assembly (Legislative) Debates*, 1948, Vol. III, p. 1783.
[2] *Loc. cit.*
[3] Nehru, *The Discovery of India*, p. 533.
[4] *Ibid.*, p. 560.

that 'the king must bow down to public opinion'.[1] Democratic institutions also were found in ancient India.

> The democratic way was not only well-known but was a common method of functioning in social life, in local government, trade guilds, religious assemblies, etc. Caste, with all its evils, kept up the democratic habit in each group. There used to be elaborate rules of procedure, election, and debate.[2]

Thus, ancient practices provided historical precedents for the development of modern democracy in India.

During the struggle for independence Nehru frequently repeated the Congress' demand for a Constituent Assembly, elected by means of an adult franchise, men and women together, so as to secure true mass representation. Nehru declared that this was the only 'proper and democratic' way to deal with the problem, because 'fundamentally the people of India should decide the Constitution of India'.[3]

> Details of Constitutions are for lawyers to make, but the fundamental basis of a constitution for a state or for the whole of India can only be one: that power and responsibility and ultimate sovereignty must rest with the people.[4]

As the fulfilment of this aspiration, the Constituent Assembly drafted, and formally adopted the Constitution of India on November 26, 1949. A Parliament representing the 'sovereign will of the people' was elected in accordance with its provisions in 1951-1952.

Reflecting on his early experiences with general elections (those of 1937), Nehru once wrote that 'Elections were an essential and inseparable part of the democratic process and there was no way of doing away with them', even though certain evils might accompany elections.[5] Nehru wanted the widest possible franchise, without any property qualification or even an educational test. The electoral machinery was necessary to democratic procedure, but as Nehru later pointed out in the Constituent Assembly debates, 'there is such a thing as

---

[1] Nehru, *Glimpses of World History*, p. 199.

[2] Nehru, *The Discovery of India*, p. 253. For other references to the democratic values found in ancient Indian traditions, *supra*, p. 19.

[3] Speech in London, February 4, 1936. *Important Speeches of Jawaharlal Nehru*, p. 299.

[4] *The Hindu*, August 28, 1946, p. 4.

[5] Nehru, *The Discovery of India*, p. 53.

too much of a democratic procedure'.[1] In supporting an amendment to the draft constitution whereby the governors of states would be nominated rather than elected, Nehru declared:

> We have still to pass through difficult times and I think we should always view things from this context of preserving the unity, the stability and the security of India and not produce too many factors in our constitutional machinery which will tend to disrupt that unity by frequent recourse to vast elections which disturb people's minds and at the same time divert a great deal of our resources towards electoral machines rather than towards the reconstruction of the country.[2]

Furthermore, it would be quite unnecessary to have an elective governor *plus* the cabinet system of government in the states.

In *Glimpses of World History* Nehru pointed out that the extension of political equality through the gradual widening of the right to vote was one of the principal trends in the development of nineteenth- and early twentieth-century democracy. This development rested on the revolutionary premise that despite obvious human inequalities, 'each person should be treated as having equal political and social value'.[3] The nineteenth-century democrats felt sure that the vote would automatically bring about equality in other matters. Nehru's socialistic criticisms were that political equality (one vote for each man), while good as far as it went, was inadequate and had failed to effect equality in other realms.

> Thus political power, which the vote was supposed to give, was seen to be a shadow with no substance, without economic power, and the brave dreams of the early democrats, that equality would follow from the vote, came to nothing.[4]

The ideas underlying the above sentence, written in 1933, had been somewhat modified by 1951, when Nehru admitted that political equality was 'the very basis on which you build up other equalities'.[5] If the individual lacked political equality he would be without the main tools by which other rights could be secured.

The idea of majority rule is of course an integral part of

---

[1] India, *Constituent Assembly Debates*, 1947, Vol. IV, p. 734.
[2] India, *Constituent Assembly Debates*, 1949, Vol. VIII, p. 455-6.
[3] Nehru, *Glimpses of World History*, p. 528.
[4] *Ibid.*, p. 529.
[5] Cousins, *Talks with Nehru*, p. 19.

4

Nehru's definition of democracy: 'If a government is in line with the thought of a majority of the people, it is a democratic government'.[1] In *Glimpses of World History* he pointed out how English utilitarianism ('the greatest happiness of the greatest number') was not quite the same as the earlier liberal democratic doctrine of equal rights for everyone. 'Democracy thus came to mean the rights of the majority.'[2] Although the idea of majority rule is essential to the functioning of democracy, Nehru emphasized that there was no mysterious wisdom to be found in the device of majority rule: 'With all my admiration and love for democracy I am not prepared to accept the statement that the largest number of people are always right.'[3] Referring to the post-partition atrocities and mass migrations in the Punjab, he commented, 'I do not blame those poor people but I do say that even democracy can go mad; democracy can be incited to do wrong'.[4]

Nehru's experience with the communal problem early led him to the conclusion that the democratic principle of majority rule, important as it was, would have to be balanced by other considerations. Definite constitutional guarantees would have to be extended for the protection of the cultural and religious rights of minorities. The Congress, Nehru asserted, was fully aware of this fact, and

> it realized that in a vast and varied country like India, a simple type of democracy, giving full powers to a majority to curb or overrule minority groups in all matters, was not satisfactory or desirable, even if it could be established.[5]

Thus Nehru's Karachi resolution on Fundamental Rights and Duties (1931) mentioned not only freedom of religion, but the protection of the culture, language and script of the minorities as well.[6] These clauses found their fulfilment in Articles 25 through 30 of the Constitution of India. The principle of majority rule is thus strictly limited in some areas by the fundamental rights of the individual and of minority groups.

[1] Nehru, *Visit to America*, p. 95.
[2] Nehru, *Glimpses of World History*, p. 531.
[3] Speech in the House of the People, February 18, 1953. *Jawaharlal Nehru's Speeches, 1949-53*, p. 252.
[4] *Loc. cit.*
[5] Nehru, *The Discovery of India*, pp. 388-9.
[6] Nehru, *The Unity of India*, p. 406.

Nehru has raised some very fundamental questions regarding the future validity of these concepts of popular sovereignty and majority rule. He has expressed concern over what he considers a trend in the modern world away from the life of the mind. Civilization has been produced by the human mind, and yet, 'strangely enough, one begins to feel that the function of the mind becomes less and less important in the modern world'.[1] Great changes, stemming from the Industrial Revolution, have produced a mechanical civilization in which other aspects of life are emphasized.

Am I right in saying that the mental life of the world is in a process of deterioration, chiefly because the environment that has been created by the Industrial Revolution does not give time or opportunity to individuals to think?[2]

Ideas are circulated through new methods of mass propaganda, and these ready-made ideas and opinions have become the modern substitute for thinking. Thus the individual becomes lost in the crowd, which dominates him 'but lacks a conscience of its own'.[3]

The problem is this: in a democracy it is this 'mass of unthinking humanity' which will govern or elect those who govern.[4] Democracy, the difficult way, requires a higher standard of human being,[5] but modern conditions are producing a lower standard. The problem becomes evident during elections in any modern state, which seem to bring out the weaknesses of democracy and human nature. 'I feel, looking not only at India but other countries too, that the processes of democratic elections bring down standards everywhere.'[6] Nehru declared that the quality of men thus chosen gradually deteriorates. The noise and din of campaign propaganda prevents people from thinking, and they therefore produce

a dictator or a dumb politician, who is insensitive, who can stand all the din and noise in the world and yet remain standing on his

[1] Speech at UNESCO Symposium, New Delhi, December 20, 1951. *Jawaharlal Nehru's Speeches, 1949-53*, p. 382.
[2] *Ibid.*, p. 386.
[3] *Supra*, p. 45.
[4] *Jawaharlal Nehru's Speeches, 1949-53*, p. 386. Cf. Ortega y Gasset, *op. cit.*, p. 34. 'In our time it is the mass-man who dominates, it is he who decides'.
[5] *Infra*, p. 64.
[6] *The Hindu*, November 28, 1951, p. 6.

two feet. He gets elected while his rival collapses because he cannot stand all this din.[1]

Modern democracy thus encourages the wrong type of political leaders, yet hopes that somehow right policies will be evolved by them. Attempts to choose the right leaders by any other method than democratically have failed dismally. The situation is a great dilemma with which the democratic state must come to grips. As the matter stands, Nehru commented, the democratic state must take 'the risk of even choosing wrong people by the right method and hope for the best'.[2]

Importance of responsible political parties. What is the place of political parties in Nehru's conception of the functioning of democracy? In his earlier writings Nehru was extremely critical of Victorian England's two-party system. Both parties had more or less the same social outlook; both were rich men's parties. European parties were based on different programmes and ideologies, but in England the class conflict (which for Nehru was a basic reality of all social, economic and political life) was never reflected in the parties. Thus the voter had little real choice. Another weakness was that the members of the parties in Parliament had little or no independence. Independence was sacrificed for the sake of party solidarity and the winning of elections. Nehru asserted that 'This solidarity and uniformity is no doubt good in its own way, but it is very far from real democracy'.[3]

By 1951, however, Nehru took a rather different view of party solidarity and discipline. In fact, he stated that the only way to function in a democracy was through strictly disciplined parties.

> Suppose our Parliament at Delhi had 500 chosen men of integrity and ability, each thinking according to his own lights, the result would be that, while they would be the chosen of the nation in regard to ability, nothing will be done by the Parliament because all the 500 will pull in 500 different directions.[4]

Not only are disciplined political parties necessary for efficient government; they alone are in a position to represent the masses.

[1] Speech at UNESCO Symposium, *op. cit.*, pp. 386-7.
[2] Speech at Madras. *The Hindu*, October 3, 1953, p. 8.
[3] Nehru, *Glimpses of World History*, p. 554.
[4] Speech at Madras. *The Hindu*, November 28, 1951, p. 6.

Individuals, however able, do not represent or are not in touch with the people, while an organized party, by the mere fact of its functioning as a party, is in contact with large masses of people whom it guides, whose thinking it influences and which in turn is affected by the people's wishes.[1]

Although the Indian National Congress has occupied a position of overwhelming predominance in the post-independence political field, Nehru has deprecated all charges that the effort is being made to create a one-party system in India. On the other hand, he has often expressed the idea that stronger opposition parties would be desirable.

The formation of separate parties either with some ideological differences or placing greater emphasis on certain matters, is a natural development to which, I for my part, have no objection whatever. In a democratic setup it is desirable that every opportunity should be given for the development of ideas and the education of the public in them.[2]

Furthermore, a stronger opposition would be good for the Congress itself. It is dangerous for any political organization to have it all one way, according to Nehru.

Although the encouragement of a few strong, responsible opposition parties might be theoretically advisable, the present critical times require, above all, stable government. Nehru wrote: '. . .there are moments when one does not think in terms of party politics, such as a war or a time sufficiently on a par with war, and if we have to face it, we must face it unitedly.'[3] A large measure of unity and national purpose is needed to meet the challenge of the disruptive forces which are at work.[4] *The Hindu* of Madras, however, took a dim view of Nehru's efforts to bring about closer co-operation between the Praja Socialist Party and the Congress in the name of national integration.

Party realignments, if they are to be effective and to correspond to realities in the country, will have to be much more thorough-going and candidly based on ideological differences. The attempt to equate the Congress with the nation will have to be given up.[5]

[1] *Loc. cit.*
[2] *The Hindu*, March 19, 1953, p. 4.
[3] *The Hindu*, July 18, 1953, p. 5.
[4] *Report to the All-India Congress Committee*, 1951, p. 18.
[5] Editorial, *The Hindu*, March 20, 1953, p. 4.

Many feel that the development of a strong opposition party is far more essential for the future of democracy in India than Nehru appears to realize.

The general elections of 1951-52 brought an overwhelming 364 seats in the House of the People to the Congress. The Communist Party received the second largest number of 26. If this situation is undesirable, what could Nehru and the Congress reasonably be expected to do about it? Nehru once asked his critics if they expected the Congress deliberately to create splits in its party organization so that a stronger opposition would emerge. The present political situation is the result of a definite historical development, and cannot be manipulated at will.

Nehru's leadership, as would be expected, has consistently carried the party in the very opposite direction, i.e., toward an even larger, stronger, and more completely dominant Congress. He has continually emphasized the role of the Congress as the agent for cementing national unity. In 1954 he wrote: 'It is still the historic destiny of the Congress to labour for the real national unity of India in the present time of crisis'.[1] He has often deprecated the tendency to think too much in terms of the British concept of parliamentary opposition, instead of facing squarely the fact of India's need for unity and stability.

There are obvious dangers in continuing this 'crisis approach' to political questions over a long period of time. The building of national unity and solidarity through one political party is an approach which history has shown to be dangerous. The basic conception of a political party functioning in a democratic state might easily be lost sight of, if the present trend in India is long continued. Nehru's overemphasis on national unity through one political party may be considered a weakness of his democratic theory.

Problems of political leadership. Representative government requires responsible political leaders as well as political parties. The problem of leadership in a democratic state is a complex one. Leaders frequently function with complete disregard for truth and ethical standards. Most politicians do not even worry themselves over the problem of truth.

[1] Nehru, *Circular to the Pradesh Congress Committees*, August, 1954.

They keep truth apart in some corner of their minds, if they keep it at all anywhere, and accept expediency as the measure of the action.[1]

But that leader who does have certain convictions regarding truth is faced with a great dilemma. If he has been charged with the responsibility of leadership, he must lead and not merely succumb to the dictates of the crowd, 'though some modern conceptions of the functioning of democracy would lead one to think that he must bow down to the largest number'.[2] The leader must not surrender his understanding of truth, and bring himself down to the level of the crowd's understanding of it. Once such compromise of truth begins, there is no end to it. The leader who starts on that path may well one day find himself among those referred to above who function solely on the basis of expediency. If he does this, the leader will prove untrue both to his own ideals and to his responsibility to lead people to the good they do not yet perceive. He will not be able to guide others along the right path of human progress.[3]

On the other hand, the leader dare not attempt to act on the personal plane alone. He must not make decisions solely on the basis of his own understanding of the truth in any particular situation. If he does this, Nehru affirmed, he will cut himself off from the very people whom he seeks to lead. The leader cannot function purely on the personal plane because of the very nature of his task. Leaders 'have to make others act, and so they have to consider the limitations of others and their understanding of and receptivity to truth'.[4] The leader's perceiving truth is not enough; he must somehow help others to perceive it too.[5] In the Constituent Assembly Nehru declared:

Then a politician or statesman, call him what you will, has to deal not only with the truth but with men's receptivity of that truth because if there is not sufficient receptivity of it from the politician's

[1] Nehru, *The Discovery of India*, p. 452.

[2] Nehru, 'Foreword' to *Mahatma*, by D. G. Tendulkar, Vithalbhai K. Jhaveri and D. G. Tendulkar, Bombay, 1951, Vol. I, p. xiii.

[3] *Loc. cit.*

[4] Nehru, *The Discovery of India*, p. 452.

[5] Nehru, 'Foreword' to *Mahatma*, *loc. cit.*

or statesman's point of view, that truth is thrown into the wilderness till minds are ripe for it.[1]

A statesman of integrity cannot function successfully in a democratic age unless he can make people believe in that truth.

Hence, there arises the need for some kind of compromise between the relative comprehension of truth in the mind of the leader and in that of the people. The leader of men 'has continually to adapt himself to his environment and to choose what he considers the lesser evil'.[2] In his discussion of the different roles in society of the uncompromising prophet and the practical leader of men, Nehru quoted with approval Liddell Hart's dictum that:

> The prophets must be stoned; that is their lot and the test of their self-fulfilment; but a leader who is stoned may merely prove that he has failed in his function through a deficiency of widsom, or through confusing his function with that of a prophet.[3]

Compromises are inevitable. Nevertheless, there are good compromises and bad ones. As Nehru put it,

> You cannot do without compromises but a compromise is a bad compromise if it is opportunist in the sense that it is not always aiming at the truth. It may be a good compromise if it is always looking at that truth and trying to take you there.[4]

This, then, is the problem of leadership in a democratic state. Nehru considered that the most unusual fact about Gandhi was the degree to which he adhered to his conception of truth and yet succeeded in influencing and moving enormous masses of men and women.[5] Nehru concluded that there was no clear answer to the problem of leadership in a democracy, and 'each individual and each generation will have to find its own answer'.[6]

As we have seen in the preceding pages, Nehru has defined democracy in terms of certain governmental institutions and

---

[1] Constituent Assembly (Legislative), March 8, 1949. India, *Constituent Assembly Debates*, 1949, Vol. II, part II, p. 1229-30.
[2] Nehru, 'Foreword' to *Mahatma, loc. cit.*
[3] Liddell Hart, *The Strategy of Indirect Approach*, Faber & Faber, London, 1941, Preface. Quoted in *The Discovery of India*, p. 456.
[4] Speech in the Constituent Assembly (Legislative), March 8, 1949. India, *Constituent Assembly Debates*, 1949, Vol. II, Part II, pp. 1229-30.
[5] Nehru, 'Foreword' to *Mahatma, loc. cit.*
[6] *Loc. cit.*

principles: popular sovereignty through representatives, elections by adult franchise, majority rule, responsible political parties and leadership. In Nehru's thought, the democratic state would cease to exist if these vital elements were destroyed. But democratic institutions and procedures are not beyond questioning, and Nehru has dealt with a number of problems arising from the application of democratic theory in the modern state.

DEMOCRACY AS ECONOMIC AND SOCIAL EQUALITY

Nehru has often defined democracy in terms of a structure of society in which economic and social equality will gradually be attained. This aspect of Nehru's conception of democracy is discussed in more detail in the chapters on 'Economic Democracy'. Here it is sufficient to indicate the broad outline of his ideas on the subject. In a sense, the attempt to present Nehru's ideas on democracy under four definitions is artificial. The four aspects are inter-related at many points, as Nehru has often pointed out. Political, economic, and social freedom could not be separated. It was an integrated conception, and there could be neither political nor economic democracy without social freedom.[1]

Writing in 1933, Nehru seemed to feel that the most important challenges to democracy lay in the existing economic structure of society. One obvious problem was that the ideology of nineteenth century democracy considered the question of economic inequality, which was made more acute by the tremendous production of new wealth, as completely outside its province. Formal democracy thus isolated itself from some of the most pressing and vital issues. Yet 'democracy means equality, and democracy can only flourish in an equal society'.[2]

A second problem, as Nehru viewed it within the frame-work of his socialism, was that in the nineteenth-century democracy political power had become the monopoly of the upper classes. The political structure was supposedly built upon the principle of equality (one vote for every man), but it was never effected in practice. Far from granting some measure of economic

[1] *Times of India*, August 15, 1954.
[2] Nehru, *Glimpses of World History*, p. 825.

equality, formal democracy did not even produce true political equality. The machinery of democracy had been exploited to maintain a class government which existed to further its own interests.[1] In other words, Nehru saw capitalism as the most basic reality of the twentieth century. He saw an essential contradiction between capitalism and democracy, and thus the capitalist system itself constituted the most serious problem confronting democracy.

> The conflict between capitalism and democracy is inherent and continuous; it is often hidden by misleading propaganda and by the outward forms of democracy, such as parliaments, and the sops that the owning classes throw to the other classes to keep them more or less contented.[2]

True democracy could be attained only through the elimination of capitalism.

Nehru's later speeches and writings indicated that he had greatly modified this oversimplified analysis of the problems confronting the modern democratic state. But he never abandoned the idea that democracy must be understood in terms of equality, social and economic equality. Almost twenty years later Nehru held that the whole purpose of the Indian Constitution, as conceived in the Directive Principles, was to move toward 'a casteless and classless society'. This was the essential purpose, although it was not stated in precisely these terms. Furthermore, 'anything that perpetuates the present social and economic inequalities is bad'.[3] Nehru asserted that the spirit of the age is for equality, although it remains unfulfilled in practice almost everywhere.[4]

The entire structure of the caste system stands today as one of the greatest obstacles to the attainment of social equality in India. Nehru regarded it as an aristocratic approach based on obsolete traditions, and wholly opposed to the democratic ideal and to modern conditions.

> In the context of society today, the caste system and much that goes with it are wholly incompatible, reactionary, restrictive, and barriers to progress. There can be no equality in status and

---

[1] Ibid., p. 935.
[2] Loc. cit.
[3] Speech in the House of the People, June 1, 1951. India, Parliamentary Debates, 1951, Vol. XII, Part II, col. 9831.
[4] Nehru, The Discovery of India, p. 532.

opportunity within its framework, nor can there be political democracy, and much less, economic democracy.[1]

Between the two conceptions of democracy and caste, conflict
is inherent, and ultimately one of them must go down before
the other.

India had to aim at a new type of society whose chief purpose
would be the welfare of the people. Such a society would require not only a new social and economic setup, but a fundamental re-orientation of human motivation.

> We have to aim deliberately at a social philosophy which seeks a
> fundamental transformation of the structure, a society which is not
> dominated by the urge of private profit and individual greed and
> where there is a distribution of political and economic power. We
> must aim at a classless society based on co-operative effort, where
> there is opportunity for all.[2]

This objective toward which society should move has been
variously described by Nehru as 'a classless society', 'economic
democracy', or 'a socialistic pattern of society'.

The linking of the term 'economic democracy' with these
other terms suggests an important distinction. When Nehru
defined democracy in terms of individual freedom, or popular
government, or social self-discipline (definitions 1, 2, and 4,
respectively), he was speaking of actual *realities* which are at
present functioning, although imperfectly; when he defined
democracy in terms of economic and social equality, he was
speaking of an ideal, a goal to be striven for. It is indeed true
that the other three aspects of democracy are also ideals, yet
the difference in degree between their present attainment and
that of economic democracy is sufficiently great to warrant
calling it a difference in kind.

The first definition of democracy was in terms of individual
freedom; the third, in terms of equality. What is the relationship between freedom and equality?

> I am not quite sure if ultimately the concept of equality can be
> co-ordinated with freedom, because when you bring equality it
> may interfere with somebody's freedom. So there is a slight con-
> flict—not a final conflict, but there is a conflict.[3]

[1] *Ibid.*, p. 254.
[2] Broadcast Speech, December 13, 1952. *Building New India*, All-India Congress Committee, New Delhi, 1954, p. 53.
[3] Nehru, *Visit to America*, p. 136.

Nehru pointed out that in the nineteenth century the concept of freedom had been preeminent; in the mid-twentieth century the idea of equality was being emphasized more.

The problem of the relationship between freedom and equality was brought to the fore in the debates on the Constitution (First Amendment) Bill of 1951 in the Indian Parliament. One section of the amendment sought to clear the way for land reforms which had been declared unconstitutional in the courts of several states.[1]

These proposed amendments cast in bold relief the tension between the Constitution's Fundamental Rights and its Directive Principles of State Policy, or in other words, the tension between the concepts of freedom and equality. The Fundamental Rights protect the right of private property: 'No person shall be deprived of his property save by authority of law', and such laws must provide for 'compensation for the property taken possession of'.[2] The Directive Principles of State Policy, on the other hand, envisage economic and social reorganization along egalitarian lines: 'The State shall, in particular, direct its policy toward securing . . . that the ownership and control of the material resources of the community are so distributed as best to subserve the common good'.[3]

Nehru, in his speech moving that the amendment bill be referred to a Select Committee, declared:

> The Directive Principles of State Policy represent a dynamic move towards a certain objective. The Fundamental Rights represent something static; their object is to preserve certain rights which already exist. Both again are right. But sometimes it might so happen that the dynamic movement and the static concept do not quite fit in with each other.[4]

The dynamic movement means changes in the existing settled relationships which the Fundamental Rights are meant to preserve. When these questions have had to be settled by the courts of the land, they have naturally laid more stress on the Fundamental Rights than on the Directive Principles of State Policy. Nevertheless, in the course of protecting individual liberty,

[1] *The Constitution of India*, Article 31A and 31B.
[2] *The Constitution of India*, Article 31, sections 1 and 2.
[3] *Ibid.*, Article 39b.
[4] Speech in the House of the People, May 16, 1951. *Jawaharlal Nehru's Speeches, 1949-53*, p. 492.

If you also protect individual or group inequality, then you come into conflict with that directive principle. If, therefore, an appeal to individual liberty and freedom is construed as an appeal for the continuation of the existing inequality, then you come up against difficulties. You become static and unprogressive and cannot change; you cannot realize the ideal of an egalitarian society which, I hope, most of us want.[1]

The great strength of the British people has been their ability to adapt their political and other institutions to changing conditions, and to do so constitutionally. Nehru declared that India also must understand the importance of a flexible constitution.[2]

This, then, is the problem of relating freedom and equality in the democratic state, as Nehru viewed it. He once remarked that he was sure the conflict between the two was not an inherent one.[3] How could this problem be met? There was no one answer; it was a question of balancing the two ideas.

Until you balance the two ideas of freedom and equality, both of which are important, and each of which has to be limited to some extent in order to co-ordinate with the other, you will not solve the problem of today.[4]

DEMOCRACY AS SOCIAL SELF-DISCIPLINE

Nehru defines democracy also in terms of a certain attitude and approach on the part of the individual and society: the way of self-discipline. It is not enough to have a political structure which may be called democratic. Democracy 'must have a background and basis in the masses of the people, in their education. . . .'[5] Democracy is essentially

A scheme of values and moral standards in life. Whether you are democratic or not depends on how you act and think as an individual or as a group. There is a fundamental approach to political and other problems which may be called democratic and there are others which are not.[6]

[1] *Ibid.*, p. 493.
[2] Speech in the House of the People, May 29, 1951. *Jawaharlal Nehru's Speeches, 1949-53*, p. 525.
[3] Speech in the House of the People, May 16, 1951. *Jawaharlal Nehru's Speeches, 1949-53*, p. 492.
[4] Speech in San Francisco, November 1, 1949. Nehru, *Visit to America*, p. 136.
[5] Speech at the All-India Newspaper Editors' Conference, September 17, 1952. *Jawaharlal Nehru's Speeches 1949-53*, p. 469.
[6] Speech in the House of the People, August 2, 1952. *Jawaharlal Nehru's Speeches, 1949-53*, p. 578.

Nehru once wrote that democracy meant freedom, but it also meant discipline, and 'we must therefore develop both the freedom and the discipline of democracy among our people'.[1] Again,

> You may define democracy in a hundred ways but surely one of its definitions is self-discipline of the community. The less the imposed discipline and the more the self-discipline the higher is the development of democracy.[2]

This self-discipline means that what is done after argument, discussion, and the general consent of the majority, is agreed to by the minority with a sense of acceptance. The minority might later challenge the decision again, but always through peaceful, democratic procedure. Democracy, with its demand for self-discipline, is thus the hard way to function in society. 'In other words,' Nehru declared, 'democracy means a higher standard of human being'.[3]

The hallmarks of democracy, defined as social self-discipline, are two: tolerance and peaceful methods. Nehru held that 'Democracy means tolerance, tolerance not merely of those who agree with us, but of those who do not agree with us.'[4] Tolerance does not mean giving up one's opinion or surrendering to another's judgment, for criticism and even opposition are also 'of the essence of democracy'.[5] Tolerance means the willingness to recognize the existence of differing points of view, and to allow the strongest view to prevail, according to established procedures.

Writing in 1940, Nehru gave a socialistic interpretation of democracy as the way of peaceful methods. He saw national life in India as one of different classes with conflicting interests. Until a classless society is achieved, 'the only known method of resolving these conflicts, other than that of force and coercion, is the democratic method'.[6] Since Independence the occasional outbreaks of violence have driven Nehru to emphasize the importance of peaceful methods in democracy.

---

[1] Nehru, *The Unity of India*, p. 77.
[2] Speech at the All-India Newspaper Editors' Conference, September 18, 1952. *Jawaharlal Nehru's Speeches 1949-53*, p. 472.
[3] Speech in Bangalore. *The Hindu*, July 14, 1951, p. 4.
[4] *Building New India*, p 34.
[5] *Presidential Address, 59th session, Indian National Congress*, January 23, 1954.
[6] Nehru, 'The Parting of the Ways,' *The Unity of India*, p. 383.

The very essence of a democratic state is its functioning in an atmosphere of peace. Problems, however difficult, are solved by peaceful methods—by discussion, negotiation, conciliation and persuasion. A decision once taken is accepted even by those who may not like it..... If this basic conception of democracy is not accepted, then democracy cannot function.[1]

Nehru declared that he did not mind any ideas whatever, however radical or revolutionary, provided that they contained a peaceful approach. But no government could tolerate a violent approach.[2] The people had every right to change laws and even governments in a democratic manner, but 'those who choose the path of violence have no faith in democracy'.[3] Nehru warned that 'if we leave off peaceful methods democracy will be the first victim and progress the second'.[4] It is only through the self-discipline of the community that permanent progress can be achieved.

Nehru's emphasis on democracy as the way of social self-discipline has firm roots in the traditions of India. The Indian social structure has always stressed the duties of the individual and the group, not their rights. The Hindu religious books 'give lists of *dharmas*, functions and duties, of various castes, but none of them contains an inventory of rights'.[5] Socially responsible action and the self-discipline of the community are thus well-known concepts in Indian thought.

Nehru was also undoubtedly influenced by Gandhi's teachings on tolerance and peaceful methods. He has made innumerable references to Gandhi's cardinal principle that ends and means are bound up together, and unethical means must inevitably distort even the highest ends. The objectives of social and political life must be sought only through non-violent means. Nehru has often deprecated the tendency among some agitators to resort to Gandhi's technique of *satyagraha* for every petty cause. The doctrine of *satyagraha* is thus perverted, and becomes in reality a denial of the meaning of democracy as social self-discipline.

[1] Nehru, *Circular to the Presidents of the Pradesh Congress Committees*, August 25, 1954.
[2] Speech in Madras. *The Hindu*, November 28, 1951. p. 6.
[3] Speech in Delhi, August 25, 1949. *Jawaharlal Nehru's Speeches 1949-53*, p. 7.
[4] Speech at Trivandrum, December 28, 1953. *Building New India*, p. 41.
[5] Nehru, *The Discovery of India*, p. 253.

By way of summary, Nehru's four definitions of democracy may be briefly reviewed. First, democracy means individual freedom. The democratic state is one in which there is freedom for the realization of human values and the creative development of personality. However, individual freedom must always be considered in the context of social responsibility. Nehru regarded the modern trend toward centralization as inevitable, but the democratic state must somehow see that it does not engulf individual freedom.

Nehru's second definition is that democracy means representative government. Popular sovereignty must be exercised through elected representatives who function by the principle of majority rule, even though the majority may sometimes be wrong. The majority should never be permitted to encroach on the fundamental rights of religious, cultural, or political minorities. Nehru expressed concern over the future of popular sovereignty in the light of the mechanical civilization which tends to impose ready-made ideas and opinions as the modern substitute for thinking. Responsible political parties are an essential element of representative government, but Nehru appears to underestimate the importance of effective opposition parties in the long-range development of democracy in India. Responsible political leaders are constantly faced with the necessity of making compromises, but Nehru feels that the distinction must be made between good compromises and bad ones.

Thirdly, democracy means economic and social equality. Nehru asserted that India's goal must be a classless and a casteless society. The definition of democracy as equality implies a dynamic movement away from the status quo, and this sometimes comes into conflict with the more static conception of democracy as freedom. Somehow the modern democratic state must balance the two.

The fourth definition is that democracy means the self-discipline of the community. The hallmarks of this social self-discipline are tolerance of differing points of view, and peaceful methods of resolving the differences or of allowing the strongest view to prevail. Disciplined functioning in society thus requires a higher type of individual; democracy is the hard way.

In Nehru's thought, each of these four definitions of

democracy is absolutely essential and indispensable. In practice, democracy would not be in operation if, for example, representative institutions were used to trample over the rights of the non-conformist individual, or to perpetuate an economic structure of vast inequality, or if the institutions were not used according to established procedures and with a measure of self-discipline. The functioning of a truly democratic state necessarily involves the application of all four aspects of democracy.

IV

FUNDAMENTAL RIGHTS IN THE INDIAN CRUCIBLE

FOR, however good the ideas of the philosophers of the eighteenth and the early nineteenth century might have been—and they are very good—the world has changed and grown beyond them within a hundred years. The world has changed mightily in the course of your generation and mine and we have seen great wars and great revolutions. We have seen the most perfect of constitutions upset, not because they lacked perfection but because they lacked reality, because they failed to deal with the problems of the day.

Speech in Parliament, 1951.

CHAPTER IV

FUNDAMENTAL RIGHTS IN THE INDIAN CRUCIBLE[1]

THIS chapter is not a comprehensive treatment of everything that Nehru has said or written on the subject of
fundamental rights. Certain rights are dealt with elsewhere; freedom of religion is mentioned in the chapter on the
secular state, and the right to property is touched upon in the
chapters on economic democracy. Here the attempt has been
made to indicate Nehru's basic approach to the question of
fundamental rights and to consider in some detail the rights of
personal liberty and freedom of the press.

GENERAL OBSERVATIONS ON FUNDAMENTAL RIGHTS

The background of Nehru's theory. As Nehru indicated in his
autobiography, his roots were still in the humanism and liberalism of the nineteenth century. The writings of Marx and Lenin
influenced him greatly, but never altered his deep convictions
concerning individual human values. As we have seen in
Chapter III, one of Nehru's important definitions of democracy
was in terms of individual freedom.[2] The end of government
should be human well-being, and this cannot be attained if the
individual's creative faculties and capacity for growth are suppressed. Nehru's humanism thus provides the background for
his ideas on fundamental rights. These ideas are based on the
concept of the inherent worth of the individual, who is regarded
as an end in himself and not merely as a means to an end.

Nehru has, however, also advanced the idea that fundamental rights must be maintained and protected for the good
of society as well as for that of the individual. He quoted the
following argument of John Stuart Mill, found in the essay
On Liberty:

But the peculiar evil of silencing the expression of an opinion is, that

---

[1] I have borrowed this expressive phrase from Dr. Eddy Asirvatham's book
Christianity in the Indian Crucible.
[2] *Supra,* p. 45.

it is robbing the human race; posterity as well as the existing generation; those who dissent from the opinion, still more than those who
hold it. If the opinion is right, they are deprived of the opportunity
of exchanging error for truth; if wrong, they lose, what is almost as
great a benefit, the clearer perception and livelier impression of
truth, produced by its collision with error . . . [1]

If the state suppresses individual creativity, it will ultimately
hinder the progress of the group and the nation. Nehru once
stated: 'Civil liberty is not merely for us an airy doctrine or a
pious wish, but something which we consider essential for the
orderly development and progress of the nation.'[2] In a slightly
broader context, Nehru pointed out that entire civilizations
have declined and decayed when thought 'lost its explosive-
ness and creative power' through rigid social systems.[3]

It is true, however, that certain evils also must necessarily be
allowed to continue in a free society. Writing of the compara-
tive decline of Indian civilization around 1000 A.D., Nehru noted:

The extreme tolerance of every kind of belief and practice, every
superstition and folly, had its injurious side also, for this perpetuated
many an evil custom and prevented people from getting rid of the
traditional burdens that prevented growth.[4]

India in this period had a strange combination, as far as fundamental rights were concerned. The individual had complete
freedom of thought and conscience, but was made to conform
strictly to social and communal regulations in his public
conduct.[5]

Fundamental rights must be preserved because the individual is important in himself, because only thus can social
progress be promoted, and also because ideas cannot usually
be suppressed successfully. When the attempt is made to crush
a contrary opinion forcibly, it usually not only survives but
prospers all the more, as history has shown.

Long experience has taught us that it is dangerous in the interest of
truth to suppress opinions and ideas; it has further taught us that
it is foolish to imagine that we can do so.[6]

[1] Nehru, *Glimpses of World History*, p. 531.
[2] Nehru, *The Unity of India*, p. 67.
[3] Nehru, *The Discovery of India*, p. 220.
[4] *Ibid.*, p. 86.
[5] *Ibid.*, p. 136.
[6] Nehru, *The Unity of India*, pp. 67-8.

It is far better to come to grips with wrong ideas in the open than to drive them underground where one can make no proper approach to them.

Nehru's great concern for fundamental rights was reflected in his speeches and writings of the pre-independence period, during which period these rights were severely curtailed. Addressing the Lucknow Congress of 1936, Nehru declared:

> A government that has to rely on the Criminal Law Amendment Act and similar laws, that suppress the press and literature, that ban hundreds of organizations, that keep people in prison without trial, and that do so many other things that are happening in India today, is a government that has ceased to have even a shadow of a justification for its existence. I can never adjust myself to these conditions; I find them intolerable.[1]

Nehru deprecated the idea that the British government was preserving law and order. Law and order, in his view, were 'the last refuge of the reactionary, of the tyrant and of him who has power and refuses to part with it'.[2] Nehru quoted from *Esprit des Lois* by Montesquieu to show that law and order, which should be the refuge of the weak and oppressed, had sometimes become a weapon of oppression wielded by the tyrannical state.[3]

Law and order usually meant the preservation of the vested interests of the ruling class, and the class government dominating Britain assured the protection of these interests, both at home and abroad. There was little or no concern for the rights of individuals outside of the ruling class. Communists also disregarded fundamental rights. For all of his attraction toward Soviet Russia, Nehru could never approve of 'the ruthless suppression of all contrary opinion, the wholesale regimentation, the unnecessary violence'.[4]

Nehru drafted a resolution on Fundamental Rights and Economic Programme which was adopted by the Karachi Congress of 1931. The first section dealt with 'Fundamental Rights and Duties', and later influenced the drafting of Part III ('Fundamental Rights') in the Indian Constitution, as it

[1] Nehru, *Toward Freedom*, p. 395.
[2] Speech at Poona, December 12, 1928. *Important Speeches of Jawaharlal Nehru*, p. 59.
[3] Nehru, *Glimpses of World History*, p. 477.
[4] *Ibid.*, p. 229.

was indeed intended to do. In the introduction to the resolution it was stated that:

> The Congress therefore declares that any constitution which may be agreed to on its behalf should provide, or enable the Swaraj government to provide, the following:[1]

A casual glance at the fourteen clauses of this section is sufficient to enable one to see the considerable influence on the later constitution; several of the clauses are as follows:

> (i) Every citizen of India has the right of free expression of opinion, the right of free association and combination, and the right to assemble peacefully and without arms, for a purpose not opposed to law or morality.
>
> (ii) Every citizen shall enjoy freedom of conscience and the right freely to profess and practice his religion, subject to public order and morality.
>
> (iv) All citizens are equal before the law, irrespective of religion, caste, creed or sex.
>
> (xiv) Every citizen is free to move throughout India and to stay and settle in any part thereof, to acquire property and to follow any trade or calling, and to be treated equally with regard to legal prosecution or protection in all parts of India.[2]

As will be seen from the reading of this resolution, Nehru's thinking on the subject of fundamental rights was steeped in the very traditions of the individualistic nineteenth-century democracy which he criticised so severely on other grounds.

In 1937 Congress ministries assumed office on the provincial level, under the provisions of the Government of India Act of 1935. For the first time the Congress was faced with a degree of responsibility for public policy, although the powers of the ministries were rigorously delimited. Nehru wrote that the removal of police censorship and the banning of books and newspapers should be a definite objective of the Congress ministries:

> We must get rid of these bans and censorships and nurture the free soil from which the life of the intellect can grow and the creative faculties can take shape.[3]

Nevertheless, thinking now more in terms of the practical

---

[1] Nehru, *The Unity of India*, p. 406.
[2] *Loc. cit.*
[3] *Ibid.*, p. 69.

problems which the Congress ministries would face, Nehru conceded that coercive action might be necessary, despite the strong desire to avoid it. 'No government can tolerate the preaching of violence and communal strife,' he wrote, and if this should take place, it would have to be forcibly curbed by 'the coercive processes of the ordinary law'.[1] Thus, the assumption of partial responsibility immediately cast the problems of freedom and order in a new light for Nehru and the Congress.

Nehru's basic approach. Needless to say, the coming of full independence and complete responsibility heightened the problem and created the need for certain adjustments in Nehru's theory of fundamental rights. The violence and the communal strife of 1947-51 constituted a new situation for which old theories were inadequate. Nehru's government acted, sternly and decisively, to curb violence and re-establish 'law and and order'. But the irony of the situation was not lost on Nehru. He frankly stated the problem when he declared in 1949:

> Here we are committed to civil liberty in its broadest form. There can be no freedom in a country without a wide extension of civil liberties. We are also interning people without trial in large numbers and some of our Provincial Governments are passing legislation of a kind to which we took the greatest objection in the old days.[2]

Nehru remarked that when people came to him complaining about restrictions of civil liberty they found 'a certain answering echo in our minds'.[3]

Nehru's solution to this conflict between freedom and order is dealt with later in more specific terms, in the discussions of the rights of personal liberty and freedom of the press. Here, two general principles are delineated, which indicate Nehru's basic approach to the problems arising from the operation of fundamental rights in modern society.

The first principle is that individual freedom is essential but carries responsibility. Nehru's emphasis on the essentiality of freedom for the creative development of the individual has already been dealt with, and need not be reiterated here.[4] But

[1] *Ibid.*, p. 68.
[2] Speech in New Delhi, March 4, 1949. *Independence and After*, p. 186.
[3] *Loc. cit.*
[4] *Supra*, pp. 45-7.

Nehru has also repeatedly emphasized that 'without responsibility freedom gradually becomes something very near licence'.[1]

> We, who have been fighting for our rights and have finally achieved them, are apt to forget that a right by itself is incomplete and, in fact, cannot last long if the obligations which accompany that right are forgotten by the nation or by a greater part of it.[2]

The irresponsible exercise of freedom inevitably undermines freedom itself, for responsibility, duties and obligations are inherent in freedom. There must be a balance of individual and social freedom. In any social group, the idea of absolute individual freedom is a meaningless abstraction. In short, 'the individual must not infringe on the freedom of other individuals'.[3]

The second principle is that self-discipline is the only alternative to imposed discipline. Freedom carries responsibilities. If the individual and the group recognize and accept these responsibilities, and act on the basis of self-discipline, well and good. If, however, this is not done, the state must inevitably resort to some kind of imposed discipline. No state can tolerate utter lack of discipline for any length of time, because it leads to chaotic conditions, and undermines the security of the state itself. Thus, there must be discipline, which 'may be self-discipline or imposed discipline or, to some extent, both'.[4]

The level of democracy may be measured by this rule, that 'the less the imposed discipline and the more the self-discipline, the higher is the development of democracy'.[5] Nehru made these remarks when addressing the All-India Newspaper Editors' Conference, and urged upon them the necessity of building up the strongest possible public opinion among the members of their profession. This would act as a check upon the irresponsible sections of the Indian press. Beyond a strong public opinion, some definite sanctions should be devised by their organization. A responsible body 'has the right to pull up any

---

[1] Speech in New Delhi, December 3, 1950, *Jawaharlal Nehru's Speeches, 1949–53*, p. 461.

[2] *Loc. cit.*

[3] *Jawaharlal Nehru's Speeches, 1949–53*, p. 504.

[4] *Ibid.*, p. 462.

[5] *Loc. cit.* T. H. Green held that in a state the fear of punishment should be necessary only to restrain that minority of citizens 'in whom civic sense is lacking, and for the occasional reinforcement of the law-abiding principle in others'. *Principles of Political Obligation*, p. 424.

member of that profession, if he is flagrantly wrong'.[1] The principle of self-discipline must be applied not only to the press, but to political parties, religious organizations and other groups, and ultimately to every individual who seeks to exercise his fundamental rights in a free society. Otherwise, discipline must inevitably be imposed by the state.

THE RIGHT OF PERSONAL LIBERTY

Few political leaders of modern times have had such an intimate experience with the denial of personal liberty as Jawaharlal Nehru. Altogether he spent more than nine years in jail. Nehru wrote in his autobiography:

> The years I have spent in prison! Sitting alone, wrapped in my thoughts, how many seasons I have seen go by, following one another into oblivion! . . .How many yesterdays of my youth lie buried here![2]

Writing from Ahmadnagar Fort prison he complained bitterly that scores of thousands of Indian patriots lay in prison or internment camps without trial. Italian prisoners of war kept in India were to a degree protected by the Geneva Convention, but no such law governed the conditions under which the Indian *detenus* had to exist.[3]

Reflecting on the basic nature of the state, Nehru wrote on another occasion that civilization had undoubtedly been built up on co-operation and mutual collaboration. But in times of crisis, when the state fears some danger, the peaceful aspects are

> . . . subordinated to the primary function of the State—self-protection by force and violence. The army, the police, the prison come into greater prominence then, and of the three the prison is perhaps the nakedest form of a State in miniature.[4]

Nehru found it curious that the governing group in a state, which was based on extreme violence, should object *on moral grounds* to the violence of others. The state might well object on practical grounds of self-protection, but he saw no justification

[1] Speech in New Delhi, September 3, 1950. *Jawaharlal Nehru's Speeches, 1949-53*, p. 462.
[2] Nehru, *Toward Freedom*, p. 353.
[3] Nehru, *The Discovery of India*, p. 4.
[4] Jawaharlal Nehru, *India and the World*, George Allen and Unwin, London, 1936, pp. 143-4.

for the state to surround its actions with a halo of morality. State violence was preferable to private violence chiefly because 'one major violence is far better than numerous petty private violences', and also because state violence tended to be more orderly.[1]

Two of the clauses of the Karachi Resolution, drafted by Nehru, touched on the right of personal liberty.

(viii) No person shall be deprived of his liberty, nor shall his dwelling or property be entered, sequestered, or confiscated, save in accordance with law;

(xiv) Every person is free to move throughout India and to stay and settle in any part thereof, ... [2]

These were the ideals which had to be applied to Indian conditions. But the conditions prevailing in different parts of India from 1947 through 1951 were hardly conducive to the maintenance of maximum liberty.

Conditions of disorder and violence. Most of the violent and anti-social activities during this period were carried out by three main types of individuals and groups: (1) communist, (2) communal, and (3) *jagirdari* elements. In February 1949 the Communist Party of India tried to precipitate a railway strike, just as a famine was developing in Gujarat and Kutch. The communists, Nehru asserted, had little or no interest in bettering the lot of the workers, but wanted to use the strike as a weapon to create a state of chaos in the country, through which their party interests could be furthered. By paralyzing the railways, they sought to hinder the alleviation of famine conditions, and thus produce a breakdown of the administration and mass uprisings.

Nehru declared that while interfering with the freedom of action of others, the Communist Party 'demands full freedom for itself to carry on its own anti-social and disruptive activities'.[3] Action by the government to check these disruptive

---

[1] *Loc. cit.* Nehru was perhaps influenced at this point by the anarchists, whose writings he had read. While Nehru in 1936 seemed to agree that there was no *moral* justification for the coercive authority of the state, he did (unlike the anarchists) perceive its advantages for society. Nehru did not pursue further this line of reasoning, which logically conflicted with both his socialist doctrines of that time, and with his later emphasis on the state as providing the conditions for the creative development of personality.

[2] Nehru, *The Unity of India*, pp. 406–7.

[3] India, *Constituent Assembly (Legislative) Debates*, 1949, Vol. II, Part. I, pp. 1110-11.

activities was protested as an infringement of civil liberties, and the communists started organizations for the 'protection' of these liberties. Defending the Government's action in arresting some 870 persons who were attempting to precipitate the strike, Nehru declared in the Constituent Assembly that they were anxious to maintain full civil liberties in India.

> But it is not Government's conception of civil liberty to permit methods of coercion and terrorism to be practiced against the general community. It is the paramount duty of Government to give security to the people and to prevent the normal life of the community from being interfered with by such methods of violence. No government and no social life would be possible, if these methods were tolerated.[1]

Another example of communist violence took place in Telengana where the government had to contend against 'conditions approximating to a civil war', in which arms were used against the authority of the State.[2]

Several communal organizations were active in fomenting Hindu-Muslim strife and violence, both in the 1947 partition days in Delhi and throughout the Punjab, and in the mass exchange of populations between East and West Bengal in 1950. In the latter case, the city of Calcutta faced enormous problems because of the large influx of displaced persons from East Bengal. Nehru described conditions in the city as 'a state of semi-terror'.[3] Bombs were thrown at policemen, shops were looted, and tramcars were overturned. A bomb was thrown which killed several people in a public meeting which Nehru was addressing. Communal groups were definitely implicated in these terroristic activities.

Nehru also mentioned *jagirdari* elements as being responsible for violence and anti-social activities, although their actions were more localized and on a much smaller scale than those of either communist or communal groups. The *jagirdars*, large landholders, bitterly opposed the land reforms which the Congress Governments were seeking to carry out in Rajasthan and Saurashtra. Several men were killed in these states by *jagirdari* elements, Nehru stated, so that they would not vote for the Congress.

[1] *Loc. cit.*
[2] Speech in the House of the People, August 2, 1952. *Jawaharlal Nehru's Speeches, 1949–53*, p. 579.
[3] *Ibid.*, p. 582.

It was openly proclaimed in posters—they did not believe in hints—
that any one who voted for the Congress would be killed.[1]

The conditions of disorder and violence fomented by these three
types of groups constituted the social context in which individual freedom would have to be limited.

Individual freedom and social stability. The Preventive Detention
Act of 1950 was enacted by the Indian Parliament to provide
means of dealing with the above-mentioned conditions effectively and expeditiously. The original Detention Act was very
severe, as Nehru admitted later, and was therefore amended in
1951 and again in 1952. The Act, as amended, grants the Central Government and State Governments power to make orders
for the detention of persons under certain circumstances. This
power may be exercised in order to prevent a person from acting in a way prejudicial to: (1) the defence and security of
India, or her relations with foreign states; (2) the security of
the State, or the maintenance of public order; (3) the maintenance of supplies and services essential to the public.[2]

Orders can be made by district magistrates, or commissioners
of police or collectors in certain states. The person in respect of
whom the order has been made may be detained,

> in such place and under such conditions as to maintenance, dis-
> cipline and punishment for breaches of discipline, as the appropriate
> Government may, by general or special order, specify.[3]

The person detained must be informed within five days of the
grounds on which the order has been made, and must be given
the earliest opportunity of making a representation against the
order.[4] The case of the detained person is to be referred to an
Advisory Board consisting of three persons who are, have been,
or are qualified to be appointed as judges of a High Court.[5]
The appropriate government must then present to the Advisory
Board the grounds on which the detention order was made. It
is specifically stated that no legal practitioner may appear
before the Advisory Board on behalf of the person detained.
The Board must report 'as to whether or not there is sufficient

[1] *Ibid.*, p. 585.
[2] *The Preventive Detention Act*, No. iv of 1950 (as modified up to November 1,
1952). Article 3 (a). Government of India Press.
[3] *Ibid.*, Article 4 (a).
[4] *Ibid.*, Article 7.
[5] *Ibid.*, Article 8.

cause for the detention of the person concerned'.[1] The detention order shall be confirmed or revoked by the appropriate government in accordance with the report of the Advisory Board. If the detention order is confirmed, the maximum period of detention is twelve months.[2]

It is obvious that several important principles, generally regarded as essential in a democratic legal system, have not been adhered to in this Act. For example, the *preventive* aspect of the procedure is apparently a clear violation of basic legal principles, for a man may be arrested and detained without any crime having been committed. The failure to permit legal counsel to represent the detained person appears to be another violation of a time-honoured legal principle. As Nehru remarked in Parliament in his reply to the debate on the Preventive Detention (Second Amendment) Bill,

> We have listened to a large number of speakers during this debate. Many of them were eloquent, others narrated individual experiences, some were even autobiographical. They enunciated democratic principles and were at pains to point out how this Bill violates all of them.[3]

Nehru's defence clearly brought into focus the practical problems arising out of the conflict between freedom and order.

The Preventive Detention Bill envisaged detention in prison (a form of punishment) of individuals without any crime having been committed. They were to be detained in order to *prevent* them from carrying out the acts mentioned in article 3.[4] This was justified on the grounds that, with respect to the organized violence being perpetrated by certain groups, the damage done would be so great as to render meaningless the action of the state after the act was committed. The community could best be protected, not by punishing the anti-social persons after the damage was done, but by restraining them from doing the damage.

Nehru defended the Bill against the criticism that a full-fledged trial should be given to be *detenus*. In the first place, he

[1] *Ibid.*, Article 10.
[2] *Ibid.*, Article 11 A.
[3] Speech in the House of the People, August 2, 1952. *Jawaharlal Nehru's Speeches, 1949–53*, p. 578.
[4] *Supra*, p. 80.

was not much impressed with the kind of justice which a full trial would produce.

> The defect really lies with the judicial structure which we have inherited from the British which entails inordinate delay and expense. However efficacious this system may be, it really proves to be unjust in the end because of the excessive delay and expense it involves.[1]

Nehru pointed out that the Advisory Board, composed of three judges of the High Court or other qualified and eminent men, would be completely independent of executive authority, and in a position to give an impartial decision. They would have the opportunity to meet the accused and question him, and would be likely to take a lenient view of his offence. If this procedure were to be converted into a semi-trial, lawyers would have to be introduced on both sides, and the judges would no longer feel the same sympathy or responsibility for the accused. Thus, the interests of the accused would be best protected by maintaining the simple procedure envisaged in the Bill.

Nehru's observation was that the Bill was criticized mostly 'in rather academic terms, in terms of the nineteenth-century concept of British democracy'.[2] There was a sense of unreality about the debate, which was conducted in terms and abstract concepts quite unrelated to the actual conditions then prevailing in India.

> We are in the middle of the twentieth century and I doubt if these concepts can apply *in vacuo* to any given situation in India. My Government and I fully accept and endorse democratic values and standards but one should avoid thinking merely in terms and phrases and clichés, forgetting in the process the principles which they represent.[3]

Nehru agreed that India had fashioned its Parliament and laws after the British pattern, to a large extent. It was therefore natural that they should look to British democratic practices as a rough kind of guide. But they should never ignore or underestimate important differences.

I must, however, point out that there is a vital difference between

---

[1] Speech in the House of the People, August 2, 1952. *Jawaharlal Nehru's Speeches, 1949–53*, p. 578.
[2] *Ibid.*, p. 579.
[3] *Loc. cit.*

our country and that compact little island with centuries-old traditions of disciplined behaviour by the citizens and above all the Rule of Law. I admire her people for it; but only a few years have elapsed since our country emerged from servitude.[1]

India was a vast country, with a large population composed of many diverse groups. India had no long traditions of democratic procedure, and had been in fact confronted by conditions of extreme disorder and violence. In the light of modern conditions, the Indian Government's handling of the problem compared favourably with that of many other governments in Asia and Europe. Nehru invited a comparison of the Government of India with authoritarian regimes, and asked, 'Can the honourable members still maintain that this measure is unduly restrictive in the modern context?'[2]

Bearing in mind the conditions in India, Nehru declared that 'the essential question remains as to where the line should be drawn between the interests of the State and those of the individual'.[3] A general rule was that in times of war, when the State itself is threatened, the demarcation should be in favour of the State. In times of peace the line should be drawn more with the interests of individual freedom in mind. This principle was generally recognized as valid. Thus, fundamental rights should never be conceived of as absolutes; their extension or restriction must necessarily vary with the circumstances.

This tension of interests arises not only in times of war; it is an inherent conflict which comes to the surface more clearly in emergencies. 'Unless the State is perfect and every individual is perfect, there is always some conflict between the freedom of the individual and the security of the State.'[4] There is no formula by which this conflict can ultimately be resolved. It is a matter of balancing the two interests. This balance cannot be settled once and for all times; it must continually be readjusted with changing conditions. The conditions prevailing in India warranted the measures provided in the Preventive Detention Bill. The situation constituted a state of

[1] *Ibid.*, p. 583.
[2] *Ibid.*, p. 580.
[3] *Ibid.*, p. 583.
[4] *Loc. cit.*

continuing emergency in which the basic foundations of the State were endangered.

> If, in the name of democracy, you want people to be incited to do wrong and the structure of a democratic State we have built up undermined, you are welcome to it. Only it is not my conception of democracy.[1]

Nehru declared that while he cherished the freedom of the individual, if the safety of the state is at stake, 'the freedom of certain individuals has to be curbed'.[2]

The main emphasis of Nehru's theory of fundamental rights is that freedom must always be limited by the circumstances prevailing in any given situation. The basic principle is undoubtedly valid, and must be recognized in any democratic theory. The weakness of Nehru's theory is that it appears to be aimed primarily at adjusting freedom to circumstances in one direction only. The conditions of violence and disorder prevailing in India in the period 1947–51 certainly warranted some limitation of traditional freedoms. The relative tranquility since 1951, on the other hand, should call for a corresponding adjustment of the extent of freedom in the opposite direction, i.e., toward enlarging it. However, in 1954 the life of the Preventive Detention Act was extended, not for one year as had previously been done annually, but for three years.

Most people in India seem to feel that the Preventive Detention Act has been used with due restraint. Nehru stated in March 1954 that the average number of persons detained under the Act at any one time in all of India would be between one hundred and two hundred. Nevertheless, the Act is an emergency measure. Such measures tend to be continued long after the emergency ceases, and then are justified on the basis of their usefulness 'in case of emergency'. Sound democratic theory and policy must take this tendency into account, and see that the state responds to changing circumstances with equal flexibility in restoring freedoms as in restricting them.

THE RIGHT OF FREEDOM OF THE PRESS

The whole conception of fundamental rights for the protection of individual liberty and freedom may be traced to the

[1] *Ibid.*, p. 582.
[2] *Ibid.*, p. 583.

period of the French Revolution. This conception, according to Nehru, 'might be said to be the dominating idea of the nineteenth century, and it has continued to be a matter of fundamental importance'.[1] The freedom of the press and these other rights have continued to be of fundamental importance in Nehru's own thinking.

So, one believes in the freedom of the press, freedom of expression and other freedoms which are very important. For my part, I do think that basically it is dangerous to suppress thought and the expression of thought in any way, because this may, besides suppressing a particular good thing, produce many kinds of evil which stunt the growth of a social group.[2]

Nevertheless, however good the concepts of the eighteenth and nineteenth centuries may be, the world has changed mightily and the present age is a revolutionary one. The most perfect of constitutions have been overthrown, 'not because they lacked perfection but because they lacked reality, because they failed to deal with the real problems of the day'.[3] In the section below are considered the 'real problems of the day' relating to the exercise of freedom of the press.

The modern Indian press. In his speeches and writings Nehru has pointed out a number of conditions which he finds to be prevalent in the Indian press, and which must be considered in any meaningful discussion of freedom of the press. Nehru's interest in this matter led him to announce in Parliament that he was prepared to appoint a commission to examine the state of the press. The Press Commission was appointed in 1952, and was composed of eleven members, some representing the press. The *Report of the Press Commission* was published in 1954, and has been drawn upon in this section to provide facts and findings which substantiate Nehru's own analysis of the situation.[4]

Five conditions relating to the modern Indian press, as described by Nehru, are here considered. The first two or three could be said to apply not only to India but to other parts of the world as well; the others are specifically Indian conditions. The first condition is the general tendency of the modern

[1] Speech in the House of the People, May 16, 1951, *Jawaharlal Nehru's Speeches, 1949-53*, p. 493.
[2] Speech in New Delhi, September 17, 1952. *Ibid.*, p. 468.
[3] Speech in the House of the People, May 29, 1951. *Ibid.*, p. 524.
[4] *Report of the Press Commission*, Government of India Press, Delhi, 1954.

newspapers to regiment public opinion. The newspaper is one of the most important media of mass propaganda. Nehru sees in it potentialities for being used actually to curb the freedom of expression of the non-conformist. The press might be used 'to terrorize the public and might, to some extent, regiment public opinion', preventing the public from developing the broad tolerance of divergent views so necessary for the proper functioning of democracy.[1] In some of the democratic countries which have guaranteed constitutional freedoms this tendency is very strong.

> In those States the whole nature of the development of their mechanical civilization is such that the mind of the people becomes mechanized and regimented and you find, therefore, great countries moved by mass hysteria because the newspapers help them or for other reasons and the poor non-conformist is as badly off as if he had no fundamental right or freedom of the press or anything.[2]

This condition is of course not as serious in India as in the highly industrialized countries. But Nehru considers it a definite tendency which will have to be reckoned with in the future.

The second condition relating to the modern press is that there is an increasing degree of concentration in the press, with ownership and control in the hands of a wealthy few. This tendency is quite marked in India, and more so in certain other countries. Regarding the question of concentration of the press, Nehru pointed out that freedom, in the minds of most people, meant only lack of suppression by governmental authority. But,

> when gigantic newspaper chains spring up and undermine the freedom of the independent newspapers, when the press in India is controlled by three or four groups of individuals, what kind of press is that?[3]

Nehru disliked the tendency to form combines and trusts of newspapers because they 'defeat the very object of independent and informed criticism'.[4]

The Press Commission reported that out of a total of 330 daily newspapers, five owners controlled twenty-nine papers

[1] Speech in New Delhi, August 15, 1954.
[2] Speech in the House of the People, May 31, 1951. India, *Parliamentary Debates*, 1951, Vol. XII, col. 9796.
[3] Speech in the House of the People, May 18, 1951. *Jawaharlal Nehru's Speeches, 1949–53*, p. 511.
[4] Speech in Bombay, *The Hindu*, April 27, 1948, p. 5.

and 31.2 percent of the total newspaper circulation. Fifteen owners controlled fifty-four newspapers and 50.1 percent of the circulation. The Press Commission was somewhat perturbed by this situation.

> There can, therefore, be no denying the fact that there already exists in the Indian newspaper industry a considerable degree of concentration. We feel that there is a danger that this tendency might further develop in the future.[1]

Nehru's complaint was that press combines usually functioned in order to promote certain vested interests. The semi-monopolistic nature of these huge newspaper chains has produced a situation completely foreign to the eighteenth century, when the traditional ideas of freedom of the press were evolved.

The other aspect of the problem is that ownership and control of the press are kept in the hands of a few extremely wealthy people. This condition has made the press something quite different from what it was even fifty years ago, in Nehru's opinion. The large newspapers of the world are 'mighty organs representing an enormous financial strength behind them'.[2] No person could even start a daily newspaper in England or America unless he were a millionaire. The situation is not quite so extreme in India, although it is moving in that direction.

What are the implications of this fact for the doctrine of the freedom of the press? Freedom of the press ultimately means the freedom of the rich man to do whatever he wants to do through the press. A man with inadequate means, regardless of admirable personal qualities or qualifications, will not have much opportunity to express himself. The person of means can buy newspapers, run them or stop them, and dictate editorial policy according to his own pleasure.

> So, it may be that the freedom of the press means not so much freedom of the writer to write what he will but rather of the owner of a newspaper to see that the writer writes something that he wants him to write.[3]

---

[1] *Report of the Press Commission*, p. 309.
[2] Speech in the House of the People, May 31, 1951. India, *Parliamentary Debates*, 1951, Vol. XII, Part II, col. 9796.
[3] Speech in New Delhi, September 17, 1952. *Jawaharlal Nehru's Speeches, 1949–53*, pp. 469–70.

More and more, freedom of the press 'will be exercised by anyone who has enough money to buy up a paper'.[1]

Nehru cited the instance of a weekly newspaper which within
ten days completely reversed its editorial policy regarding matters on which it had previously taken a very strong stand. It had
every right to do so, but this merely illustrates the fact that freedom of the press meant the freedom of the gentleman who
bought up the paper to express his views. The Press Commission noted 'a general decline in the status and independence of
the editor', particularly evident in the case of daily newspapers.[2] The newspaper proprietor is increasingly arrogating
to himself areas of editorial policy-making formerly reserved to
the editor.

The third condition relating to the modern Indian press is
that certain sections of the press have descended to levels of
extreme vulgarity. Nehru has made repeated references to this
situation.

> The other day I was looking through a large number of cuttings
> from the Urdu and Hindi press. I cannot tell you how thoroughly
> ashamed I felt; I blushed with shame to read that such things
> should be printed day after day, cartoons and letterpress and the
> rest. I could not imagine anything more disgusting and obscene and
> vile.[3]

The Press Commission reported that 'yellow journalism of one
type or another is increasing in this country'[4], although it still
represents a minority of the total circulation in India. Referring to suggestive, indecent or vulgar writing, the Commission
found that 'a number of publications which deal with the film
industry appear to consider such writing an indispensable
means of making their journals popular'.[5]

Nehru has expressed concern over the growth of this type
of vulgarity, which produces an atmosphere and mental
climate in which cultural and moral standards are inevitably
lowered.

For me, it is not a political but a moral problem. How are we to

---

[1] Speech in New Delhi. *The Hindu*, June 12, 1954, p. 4.
[2] *Report of the Press Commission*, p. 333.
[3] Speech in the House of the People May 31, 1951. India, *Parliamentary Debates*,
1951, Vol. XII, Part II, col. 9797.
[4] *Report of the Press Commission*, p. 345.
[5] *Ibid.*, p. 350.

save our younger generation from this progressive degradation of the mind and spirit?[1]

Surely the doctrine of freedom of the press could not reasonably be used to encourage such vulgarity.

The fourth condition relating to the press which Nehru has pointed out, is that certain sections of the Indian press have been instrumental in the disruption of public order. The very delicate state of Hindu-Muslim relations in India during the first few years of independence has been referred to previously.[2] Certain sections of the press were actively engaged in stirring up communal discord, some being themselves motivated by communal considerations, others desiring the increased sales brought by using sensationalism in reporting on the communal situation.

Nehru, in an address to the All-India Newspaper Editors' Conference, told of one editor who had confessed to him that the paper used sensational headlines and articles because the proprietor wanted to increase sales, although the editor himself disapproved of these methods.

It certainly is not a very noble confession to make but still it is rather an extraordinary thing when the editor of a paper with a fairly wide circulation should be compelled or should say that he is compelled to write the sort of thing which is creating communal trouble in Delhi by exaggerating a minor personal incident.[3]

The Press Commission observed:

Events preceding and following the partition of the contry have left so many people with a sense of grievance against one community or the other that the newspapers have found it a lucrative business to exploit these feelings.[4]

Some sections of the anti-Hindu or anti-Muslim press have sought, and not without success, to incite people to violence against the other community. Nehru declared in 1949, 'I do not think that any interpretation of civil liberty includes the preaching of violence'.[5] Freedom of the press may not be used to justify the incitement to violence and disruption of public order.

---

[1] Speech in the House of the People, May 16, 1951. *Jawaharlal Nehru's Speeches, 1949–53*, p. 494.
[2] *Supra*, p. 79.
[3] Speech in New Delhi, September 17, 1952. *Jawaharlal Nehru's Speeches, 1949–53*, p. 472.
[4] *Report of the Press Commission*, p. 350.
[5] Speech in New Delhi, March 4, 1949. *Independence and After*, p. 187.

The last condition to be mentioned here is that certain sections of the Indian press have considerably hindered the improvement of relations with Pakistan. Nehru stated that much warlike propaganda had been carried on in East Bengal in 1950, and was largely responsible for the atmosphere of insecurity which led to the mass migrations in both directions across the border. The press in West Bengal was also partly to blame, although Nehru felt that the Pakistan press was more responsible for the situation in its early stages.

The situation in Bengal, characterized by hurried migrations, agitation for war, riots, killings and general disorder, steadily worsened. In an effort to check the drift toward catastrophe, Nehru and Liaquat Ali Khan, the Prime Minister of Pakistan, met in Delhi to seek some solution to the immediate problem. On April 8, 1950, they signed the Delhi Agreement, often referred to as the Nehru-Liaquat Pact. In this Pact the two governments agreed that they shall:

> not permit propaganda in either country directed against the territorial integrity of the other or purporting to incite war between them and shall take prompt and effective action against any individual or organization guilty of such propaganda.[1]

Nevertheless, even later there was much agitation in certain sections of the Indian press for the forcible ending of the partition.

Nehru complained that such agitation was being carried on constantly, in clear defiance of the Agreement. The difficulty was that the Government of India had pledged itself to something which it could not in law give effect to; the Agreement was in reality merely an expression of the government's intention and desire. Nehru found himself unable to give effect to his pledged word, 'primarily, because we have a noble constitution and laws which protect civil liberty in a variety of ways, even protecting uncivil liberty and licence'.[2] If the Pakistan Government says that India threatens her by talk of war, what reply could be given?

We have none except to say that we and our Government dissociate ourselves completely from this wrong and harmful

[1] Quoted by Nehru, *Jawaharlal Nehru's Speeches, 1949–53*, p. 306.
[2] *Ibid.*, p. 307.

propaganda and that we shall fight it to the utmost. That is all we can say.[1]

Nehru bitterly resented the spreading of such propaganda, which was 'endangering international relations, embarrassing the relations between the two governments and generally creating a feeling of insecurity in the country'.[2]

Five conditions relating to the modern Indian press, according to Nehru's analysis, have been considered above. It now remains to indicate Nehru's theory of freedom of the press, in the light of these problems.

Freedom of the press in the present-day context. Nehru declared that freedom of the press, to his mind, was not merely a slogan, but 'an essential attribute of the democratic process'.[3] Therefore, the imposition of restrictions on the press was fraught with grave danger for the functioning of democracy. Informed criticism was essential to it. '. . . I would rather have a completely free press with all the dangers involved in the wrong use of that freedom than a suppressed or regulated press.'[4] Nehru has on many occasions referred to the 'fullest freedom of the press' enjoyed in India, where it is 'open to any newspaper to criticize the government'.[5] The Indian Government has no official press and no government-owned or controlled newspapers.

Freedom of the press is thus necessary, and must be maintained. On the other hand, the abuses and problems dealt with in the previous section cannot be ignored.

I think of all these difficulties and wonder how we can have real freedom of the press—a real expression of opinion for or against whatever it might be, and no suppression of any real opinion provided it is not indecent or vulgar and provided it is not exploited for wrong ends.[6]

The obvious solution to the problems created by the irresponsible sections of the press, Nehru told the All-India Newspaper Editors' Conference, was the development of a strong

---

[1] *Loc. cit.*
[2] *Ibid.*, pp. 307–8.
[3] Speech in New Delhi, December 3, 1950. *Jawaharlal Nehru's Speeches, 1949–53* p. 461.
[4] *Loc. cit.*
[5] Speech in the House of the People, February 16, 1951. India, *Parliamentary Debates*, 1951, Vol. VIII, Part II, col. 2987.
[6] Speech in New Delhi, September 17, 1952. *Jawaharlal Nehru's Speeches, 1949–53*, p. 470.

self-discipline among the members of the newspaper profession. The main organs of the Indian press had displayed fairly high standards, while some few had behaved with complete irresponsibility. Nehru urged upon the Conference the desirability of organizations such as theirs forming

> such a strong body of opinion among those who are responsible for the newspapers that any back-slider can be pulled up; or, at any rate, it can be made known to the public that the person concerned is not acting rightly.[1]

This self-discipline was the only real alternative to governmental intervention, for 'unless self-discipline develops or standards grow, some kind of standard has to be imposed'.[2] Unfortunately, the press was in an undeveloped state in India, and it was necessary to resort to more of imposed discipline, although 'it does not fit in with the democratic way of life and should not be unduly encouraged'.[3]

Common sense dictates that there must be some limitations on freedom of the press. Obviously, society could not tolerate a noted gangster preaching and advocating gangsterism, simply because society wanted to maintain freedom of the press. There is no such thing as complete, one hundred percent freedom for the individual, as soon as he associates himself with others in a social group.

> In a democratic society, the concept of individual freedom has to be balanced with social freedom, and the relations of the individual with the social group.[4]

This fact is well illustrated in the Indian Constitution. The basic concept is given in Article 19 (1) (a): 'All citizens shall have the right to freedom of speech and expression.' But, clause (2) of the same Article (before it was amended in 1951) said:

> Nothing in sub-clause (a) of the clause (1) shall affect the operation of any existing law insofar as it relates to, or prevents the State from making any law relating to, libel, slander, defamation, contempt of court or any matter which offends against decency or morality or which undermines the security of, or tends to overthrow, the State.

---

[1] Speech in New Delhi, December 3, 1950. *Ibid.*, p. 460.
[2] Speech in New Delhi, September 17, 1952. *Ibid.* p. 472.
[3] *Loc. cit.*
[4] Speech in the House of People, May 18, 1951. *Ibid.*, p. 504.

Clause (2) thus gives the social dimension of, and consequent restriction on, the individual's right of freedom of expression.

Nehru declared, 'Every freedom in this world is limited, limited not so much by law as by circumstances'.[1] The freedom of the press cannot be considered in a vacuum, but in relation to a set of circumstances. In time of war, freedom of the press is suspended. Under other circumstances, the same principle may be applied differently in different countries. Nehru summed up his position by commenting, 'I don't think that exactly the same type and extent of freedom can be applied in all circumstances at all times or in all countries; we have always to adjust ourselves to a certain set of circumstances'.[2] And, in a speech in 1951 on the bill to amend the Constitution, Nehru asserted that circumstances in India were critical; the country was 'face to face with grave national problems and questions of life and death and survival'.[3]

So, in this critical stage where there is always the question of survival, we cannot function loosely, inefficiently, without discipline, without responsibility, without thinking of our obligations.[4]

Circumstances, in Nehru's judgment, were such as to warrant granting Parliament further power to control the press by future legislation.

The Constitution (First Amendment) Bill of 1951 contained a number of proposed amendments, among them a revision of Article 19 (2) quoted above.[5] The final form of the amended clause (2) granted the State power to legislate reasonable restrictions on the freedom of speech and expression in the interests of friendly relations with foreign states, public order, or in relation to incitement to an offence. These were the three new subjects listed in addition to those given in the orginal clause (2).

The two phrases 'public order' and 'incitement to an offence', may be considered together. The necessity for the latter phrase, Nehru asserted, arose because the Bihar High Court had held that even murder or like offences could be preached under protection of the right of freedom of speech and expression. The background of disorder and violence during the immediate

[1] Speech in the House of the People, May 29, 1951. *Ibid.*, p. 504.
[2] Speech in New Delhi, September 17, 1952. *Ibid.*, p. 470.
[3] Speech in the House of the People, May 16, 1951. *Ibid.*, p. 496.
[4] *Loc. cit.*
[5] *Supra*, p. 92.

post-independence period has already been explained.[1] The role played by certain sections of the Indian press in the disruption of public order has also been alluded to.[2] Nehru's determination to deal effectively with these conditions was expressed when he declared:

> I want to be perfectly fair to this House and to the country in declaring that, if I am responsible and the Government is responsible, anything that goes to disrupt the community, anything that creates communal discord in this country will be put down with a heavy hand.[3]

The Government should allow the fullest freedom to people of all groups to preach their doctrines, whether it agreed with them or not, provided it does not lead to violence. But if the conditions referred to above should recur on a large scale due to incitements to violence, 'the country will go to pieces and the Constitution with it'.[4]

These conditions were a definite threat to the security of the state. And every state must have the right of defending itself against 'an external enemy or an internal enemy, and freedom has to be limited for that reason'.[5] This is an inherent right of the state which no constitution can take away; 'nothing in the Fundamental Rights can take away that right, because it is the basic right of the state'.[6] Furthermore, none of the fundamental rights can survive if the state goes down under the blows of the undemocratic forces at work.

> At the same time, while we want freedom, freedom of the press or freedom of speech or freedom of anything, we have to remember that the nation must remain free; the individual must be free and the country must be free.[7]

These amendments, Nehru stated, were an attempt at keeping alive the democratic process, yet meeting the dangers arising out of present conditions.

Because if you do not allow yourself that flexibility it is possible that

---

[1] *Supra*, pp. 78-80.
[2] *Supra*, p. 89.
[3] Speech in the House of the People, May 29, 1951. *Jawaharlal Nehru's Speeches, 1949–53*, p. 527.
[4] *Loc. cit.*
[5] Speech in the House of the People, May 18, 1951. *Ibid.*, p. 504.
[6] *Ibid.*, p. 506.
[7] Speech in the House of the People, May 29, 1951. *Ibid.*, p. 528.

the very freedoms that we are so anxious to preserve may themselves fade away before some other attack.[1]

The above were the arguments advanced by Nehru in support of the phrases 'public order' and 'incitement to an offence' being included in Article 19 (2).

In short, freedom of the press must be limited so that the state can protect its internal security from violence and disruption. Such limitation is justified both from the point of view of the basic right of a state to defend itself, and from the point of view of freedom of the press itself, continuance of which depends on the survival of the democratic state.

The Amendment Bill also sought the inclusion of a phrase enabling the State to frame legislation imposing reasonable restrictions on freedom of expression in the interests of 'friendly relations with foreign states'. In the previous section, the considerable harm done to Indo-Pakistan relations by irresponsible elements of the press has been discussed.[2]

Relations with Pakistan were undoubtedly uppermost in the minds of Nehru and his colleagues when the amendment was drafted. Nehru assured the Indian Parliament that there was no desire to stifle criticism of foreign policy, either that of the Government or of any country. But the State could not tolerate the press becoming the medium of incitements to war, and simply wait for the war to come. Any extreme hostility in the Indian press towards a foreign country, if continued over a period of time, might lead to a dangerous deterioration of relations with that country.

In the present delicate state of world affairs, words count, and a wrong word may create a grave international situation. In particular, defamatory attacks on leading personalities often create tensions which cannot easily be relieved. The State must have the power to deal with such conditions when they arise.

We would, indeed, be helpless spectators of a steadily deteriorating situation unless this House is armed with the authority to deal with it in good time.[3]

No state, despite its concern for the individual's freedom, could

[1] Speech in the House of the People, May 31, 1951. India, *Parliamentary Debates*, 1951, Vol. XII, Part II, cols. 9799–9800.
[2] *Supra*, pp. 90-1.
[3] Speech in the House of the People, May 16, 1951. *Jawaharlal Nehru's Speeches, 1949–53*, p. 498.

submit to 'actions which may result in war and wholesale destruction'.[1] It is, again, a basic right of the state to prevent
anything happening which will lead to war. Nehru declared:
'We cannot imperil the safety of the whole nation in the name
of some fancied freedom which puts an end to all freedom'.[2]
Freedom of the press, and indeed all the freedoms of the individual, must be balanced by the freedom of society.

In concluding the present chapter, the main elements of
Nehru's thought on fundamental rights may be briefly summarized. His basic ideas on the subject stem from his nineteenth century humanist liberal presuppositions. The individual
is important in and of himself, and can only develop fully his
potentialities in an atmosphere of freedom. Individual freedom
is also important from the point of view of the state, for its progress and advancement will be retarded if creative thinking is
stifled. Nehru's basic approach can be summed up in two propositions. First, individual freedom is essential but carries with
it responsibilities. Secondly, if the responsibilities of freedom
are not accepted on the basis of self-discipline, the state must
resort to an imposed discipline. The choice is never between
discipline and the absence of discipline: it can only be between
kinds of discipline, either self-imposed or imposed by society.

Changing conditions necessitate the periodical re-examination
and re-interpretation of fundamental rights. Nehru dealt with a
number of situations in independent India which pointed to
the necessity of certain restrictions on traditional democratic
freedoms. Conditions of disorder and violence, partly created
by communist and communal groups, threatened the basic
stability of the state. The Preventive Detention Act sought to
prevent the disruption of public order; it was not enough to
punish the offenders after the damage was done. But this Act
involved a different approach to the traditional right of freedom
from arbitrary arrest and detention. Nehru defended the Act,
not only as necessary for the security of the state, but also as
containing satisfactory safeguards for the protection of the
individual.

Surveying the modern Indian press, Nehru found a number

[1] Speech in the House of the People, May 18, 1951. *Ibid.*, p. 506.
[2] Speech in the House of the People, May 29, 1951. *Ibid.*, p. 529.

of conditions which necessitated a rethinking of freedom of the press. He found that there was a general tendency for the modern newspaper to regiment public opinion. Thus the press had potentialities for being used actually to curb the freedom of expression of the non-conformist. Secondly, Nehru asserted that there was a large and increasing degree of concentration in the press, with ownership and control in the hands of a wealthy few. Freedom of the press thus ultimately meant the freedom of the rich man to do whatever he wanted to do through the press. Thirdly, Nehru declared that certain sections of the press in India had descended to levels of extreme vulgarity, which was creating a significant moral problem within the country. Fourthly, some sections of the Indian press had been instrumental in the disruption of public order, especially with respect to the delicate matter of Hindu-Muslim relations. Lastly, Nehru pointed out that some Indian newspapers had considerably hindered the improvement of relations with Pakistan, by their constant attacks on Pakistani officials, and in some extreme cases by urging the forcible reversal of the partition of the country.

In view of such conditions, Nehru urged that freedom of the press could not be interpreted in the abstract terms of European eighteenth-century theory. It had to come to grips with the real problems of India in mid-twentieth century. The Constitution (First Amendment) Bill of 1951, which Nehru defended in Parliament, granted the State additional power to legislate reasonable restrictions on the freedom of speech and expression. The restrictions were to be exercised in the interests of maintaining friendly relations with foreign states, public order, and in relation to incitement to an offence. Nehru emphasized that in each generation a new balance must be struck between the freedom of the individual and the freedom of society.

V

ECONOMIC DEMOCRACY: THE OBJECTIVE

THEREFORE, your objective must be to put an end to all differences between class and class, to bring about more equality and a more unitary society—in other words, to strive for economic democracy. We have to think in terms of ultimately developing into a classless society. That may still be a far-off ideal; I do not know. But we must, nevertheless, keep it in view.

Speech in Parliament, 1952.

CHAPTER V

ECONOMIC DEMOCRACY: THE OBJECTIVE

ECONOMIC democracy means the application of the democratic principle of equality to the economic structure of
society. The consideration of Nehru's ideas on economic
democracy leads us directly to the subject of socialism, the
source of these ideas. The first part of this chapter deals with
the development of Nehru's socialism, the second with Nehru's
ideas on the goal of economic democracy. Chapter VI is concerned with the approach to these economic objectives.

THE DEVELOPMENT OF NEHRU'S SOCIALISM

The impact of Marxism. As a law student of about twenty-one
years of age, Nehru was vaguely attracted to the Fabians and
socialistic ideas in general. These ideas gradually receded into
the background as the nationalist movement claimed an increasing measure of his attention and loyalty. Nehru's revision-
ist socialism of the present time has much in common with the
thought of the Fabians, but he reached that position somewhat
independently. It was the thought of Marx and Lenin which
first brought him to a real commitment to socialism. In his
Marxist-inclined writings of the early 1930s Nehru gave scant
attention to the Fabians, and criticized their moderation and
conservatism. 'Even the British brand of socialism became the
most moderate of all. Fabianism this was called . . .'[1] The
Fabians were liberal intellectuals having nothing to do with the
workers, and advocated 'a very mild programme of distant
change'.[2] Nehru mentioned George Bernard Shaw as an early
Fabian, and referred to Sidney Webb's famous phrase, 'the inevitability of gradualness'.[3] The whole temper of Fabianism
seemed completely out of keeping with both Nehru's dynamism
and his Marxist ideas. Furthermore, the socialists of the British
Labour Party sometimes came under Nehru's condemnation for

---

[1] Nehru, *Glimpses of World History*, p. 535.
[2] *Ibid.*, p. 540.
[3] *Loc. cit.*

their part in British imperialism.[1] However, he did infrequently quote the writings of individual Fabians; there is one brief quotation from Harold J. Laski and one from R. H. Tawney in *Glimpses of World History*, and one from the latter ('that brilliant English writer') in *Toward Freedom*.[2]

Nehru's indebtedness to Marxian theories can be seen in three major areas, which are outlined here. He found in Marxism (1) a philosophy of history which gave meaning to the historical process; (2) a scientific approach to economic and social problems; and (3) a moral concern for the downtrodden masses which coincided with his own idealism.

The philosophy of history provided by Marxism made a deep impression on Nehru's outlook.

> A study of Marx and Lenin produced a powerful effect on my mind and helped me to see history and current affairs in a new light. The long chain of history and of social development appeared to have some meaning, some sequence, and the future lost some of its obscurity.[3]

He recorded in his autobiography that the theory and philosophy of Marxism 'lighted up many a dark corner of my mind'. The Marxist philosophy of history proved to be not only intellectually satisfying, but also very useful as a weapon in the fight for independence. Imperialism was interpreted as the last gasping effort of a decadent capitalism about to be swept away by the onward march of world socialism. Inexorable historical forces had already doomed the British *raj* in India.

Secondly, Nehru saw in Marxism a scientific approach to economic and social problems. Nehru's strong attachment to, and faith in, the scientific method has already been alluded to. The appeal of Marxism was that it was *scientific*. *Das Kapital*, Nehru wrote, was a 'purely scientific work', for Marx had dealt with his material 'dispassionately and scientifically, avoiding all vagueness and idealism'. Marx's extraordinary degree of insight into social phenomena 'was apparently due to the scientific method he adopted'. Nehru asserted that 'It was the essential freedom from dogma and the scientific outlook of Marxism that

[1] Nehru, *Toward Freedom*, p. 225. *Fabianism and the Empire: A Manifesto by the Fabian Society*, ed. Bernard Shaw, 1900, urged that Fabians must 'accept the Empire'.
[2] *Glimpses of World History*, pp. 934, 559. *Toward Freedom*, pp. 268-9.
[3] Nehru, *The Discovery of India*, p. 17.

appealed to me'.[1] This 'essential freedom from dogma' is a quality which few have claimed to find in communist theory.

Thirdly, Nehru found in Marxism a moral concern for the downtrodden masses which coincided with his own idealism. Nehru's experience in 1920 of discovering for himself the utter wretchedness in which peasant India existed has already been described. Because of his growing sensitivity to India's poverty, Nehru was attracted to a philosophy which took the problem seriously.

> But we have always to bear in mind the terrible costs of not changing the existing order, of carrying on as we do today with our enormous burden of frustrated and distorted lives, starvation and misery, and spiritual and moral degradation.[2]

Although Nehru belittled his earlier vague ideas about socialism because they were more humanitarian than scientific, there is no doubt but that 'scientific' Marxism also held a moral appeal for him.

Nehru pointed out that his adherence to the theories of socialism was never so complete as to include the fine points of doctrinal differences, which he mostly ignored. 'And so while I accepted the fundamentals of the socialist theory, I did not trouble myself about its numerous inner controversies.'[3] Nehru considered that life was too illogical to be forced into any rigid doctrinal mould or pattern. Nevertheless, one who reads his writings of the early 1930s is impressed with the comprehensiveness of Nehru's Marxian ideas. If he accepted only the fundamentals of the socialist theory, it is also true that he accepted almost all of the fundamentals, and with the utmost conviction. In 1936 he declared: 'Socialism is thus for me not merely an economic doctrine which I favour; it is a vital creed which I hold with all my head and heart'.[4]

An important reservation which Nehru made was that he did not consider Marxism a final dogma which could not be varied. It provided the basic framework for the understanding of economic and social phenomena, both past and present, but its details could not be applied everywhere unthinkingly.[5] In

[1] Nehru, Glimpses of World History, p. 539. Toward Freedom, pp. 349, 230.
[2] Nehru, Toward Freedom, p. 346.
[3] Nehru, The Discovery of India, p. 19.
[4] Presidential address to Congress, April 1936. Nehru, Toward Freedom, p. 401.
[5] Nehru, Glimpses of World History, p. 548.

particular, Nehru was quite sure that socialism would have to be adapted to the special conditions existing in India.

In the biographical sketch, several events were referred to which came as psychological shocks to Nehru during the period from 1936 to 1945.[1] The death of his wife, disagreements with Gandhi, friction in his relations with other Congress leaders, the horrors of World War II and the U.S.S.R.'s opportunist role in it, all combined to produce a sense of disillusionment in which many former values were questioned. Gradually the more rigid parts of his socialist ideology were weakened and modified. The attainment of independence and the responsibility of high public office probably reinforced the trend to seek less radical solutions to the country's problems.

Nehru's socialism: 1935 and 1955. It is instructive to compare Nehru's ideas as of 1935 on the various aspects of socialist thought with his ideas of twenty years later. This comparison clearly reveals the very considerable changes that had developed in his political philosophy. The years 1935 and 1955 have been chosen arbitrarily to represent two rather distinct periods in Nehru's political thinking. The quotations used below may vary from these two dates a few years either way.

First of all, in 1935 Nehru was quite sure that the world was faced with a clear-cut choice between socialism and capitalism. Nehru tended to see economic and social problems in a black-and-white perspective, and the black, represented by capitalism-imperialism was almost totally unrelated to the white socialism-nationalism. The tone of his thinking was indicated in his autobiography when he wrote tersely, 'a clash of interests seems inevitable. There is no middle path. Each one of us will have to choose his side'.[2] The possibility of accepting a basically capitalistic structure and gradually reforming it was specifically precluded.

> Reformism was an impossible solution of any vital problem at a critical moment when the basic structure had to be changed, and however slow the progress might be later on, the initial step must be a complete break with the existing order, which had fulfilled its purpose and was now only a drag on future progress.[3]

[1] *Supra*, pp. 30-1.
[2] Nehru, *Toward Freedom*, p. 347.
[3] *Ibid.*, p. 230.

The situation in India, and in the world, demanded a revolutionary approach to the problems of society.

In 1955, Nehru rejected the idea that the question could be framed in terms of a simple choice between two rival economic systems. In the first place, he pointed out that capitalism has been greatly modified, and has become something 'completely divorced from the old style capitalism'.[1] Those who present the problem as a simple question of capitalism or socialism demand a choice 'between Soviet Russia and something which does not exist anywhere in the world'.[2] Nehru opposed the resolution of Kazi Syed Karimuddin in the Constituent Assembly which stated: 'This Assembly is of the opinion that the economic pattern of this country shall be a socialist economy . . . '[3] The mere adoption of the term 'capitalism' or 'socialism' does not solve any economic problem, but simply indicates 'a certain approach in understanding and in trying to find a solution to that problem'.[4] Any method which 'delivers the goods' could be used, and 'that method need not necessarily be an extreme method belonging to either of these two rival ideologies', but could be something in between.[5] This middle way or 'mixed economy' which Nehru favours for India, is described in the next chapter.

Secondly, Nehru in 1935 was acutely aware of the class struggle, in accordance with the Marxian theories. He wrote that 'Class Struggles are inherent in the present system'.[6] Present society was built upon a relationship of conflicting interests; the interests of the owning classes were unalterably opposed to those of the masses—it was factory-owner against worker, landlord against peasant. All attempts to smooth over this essential conflict were superficial, and served only to confuse the basic issue. The conflict would continue until the triumph of the oppressed over the owning classes would pave the way for a classless society.

[1] Speech in New Delhi, March 4, 1949. Nehru, *Independence and After*, p. 190.
[2] Speech in New Delhi, December 26, 1950. *Jawaharlal Nehru's Speeches, 1949–53*, p. 16.
[3] Speech in the Constituent Assembly (Legislative), February 17, 1948. Nehru, *Independence and After*, p. 163.
[4] Speeches in the House of the People. India, *Parliamentary Debates*, 1951, Vol. IX, Part II, col. 4541.
[5] Speech in New Delhi, March 4, 1949. Nehru, *Independence and After*, p. 190.
[6] Nehru, *The Unity of India*, p. 118.

In 1955, however, Nehru's great concern was national unity. Many divisive forces were at work in India—communalism, casteism, provincialism, and others. In the light of these circumstances, Nehru tended to emphasize more the common interests of all classes in developing the resources of the country. The concept of class conflict, while still present, had been toned down in order to allow for greater stress upon the peaceful, democratic solution of problems arising from varying class interests.

> We know that there are class divisions and struggles and that vested interests resist any change to their disadvantage. Any attempt at reform, whether political or social, brings about a clash of these conflicting interests. It is not by denial or non-recognition of these conflicting interests that we proceed. But, at the same time, we do not encourage and intensify these conflicts because we are convinced that ultimately the surest and the best way of solving them is through peaceful methods and by a friendly approach.[1]

Speaking to the Labour Ministers' Conference in New Delhi, Nehru urged that strikes and lockouts were undesirable methods of settling industrial disputes, since they hindered production. Before they could resolve the conflicts about the division of wealth, they first had to create the wealth. They should not think of labour and capital as two different opposing camps. The interests of both coincided at many points, and especially in the need for greater production.[2]

Thirdly, Nehru in the earlier period seriously doubted that socialism could ever be introduced in a country by the normal processes of democracy. The reason was that the class struggle mentioned above was inherent in the capitalist system, and 'the attempt to change it and bring it in line with modern requirements meets with the fierce opposition of the ruling or owning classes'.[3] The failure of the democratic process to bring about vital changes in economic conditions is not caused by those who work for these changes, for they accept the democratic method, but

> When this method threatens to affect great vested interests and privileged classes, these classes refuse to accept the democratic process and rebel against it.[4]

[1] Nehru, *Report to the All-India Congress Committee*, 1955, p. 4.
[2] *The Hindu*, November 14, 1954, p. 5.
[3] Nehru, *The Unity of India*, p. 118.
[4] Nehru, *Toward Freedom*, p. 419.

For these reactionary classes, 'democracy means their own domination and the protection of their special interests'.[1] The democratic method has numerous triumphs to its credit, but has not yet succeeded in resolving this conflict, for the class which controls the state power will not give it up merely because the majority demands it.[2]

In 1955 Nehru asserted that the attainment of the socialist state must be sought only by means of the democratic process, and furthermore, that this was the only way to build up a socialist state on a firm foundation.

We must aim at a classless society, based on co-operative effort, with opportunities for all. To realize this we have to pursue peaceful methods in a democratic way.[3]

Economic planning in India, Nehru declared, was being done not only under a democratic constitution but with certain democratic objectives in view.

Therefore, howsoever much we may socialize our economy, we do want to keep democracy there. There is an obvious tendency in too much collectivism for democracy to go by the board.[4]

Nehru was determined that this should not happen in the case of India. He pointed out that the Planning Commission had to function under the self-imposed limitation of a democratic setup enshrined in the Constitution and in Parliament. Nevertheless, Nehru declared, 'I do not think it would be right to say that democratic functioning necessarily means limitations'.[5] Democratic functioning necessitated a more complicated procedure and took a longer time, but justified itself in that 'things are built on a firm foundation . . . and built with due consideration for the individual'.[6]

---

[1] *Loc. cit.*

[2] Nehru, *India and the World*, pp. 182–3. Had Nehru followed this line of reasoning to its logical conclusion, he would probably have become a Marxist revolutionary. The fact that he did not, gives added emphasis to a point already made, namely, that for Nehru socialism could not be regarded as more than a theoretical question until the attainment of independence. By the time independence was won, Nehru was no longer sceptical of the possibilities of democratic progress toward socialism.

[3] Radio address, December 31, 1952. *Jawaharlal Nehru's Speeches, 1949–53*, p. 103.

[4] Speech in New Delhi. *The Hindu*, March 8, 1953, p. 7.

[5] Speech in the House of the People, December 15, 1952. *Jawaharlal Nehru's Speeches, 1949–53*, p. 92.

[6] *Loc. cit.*

The above discussion might very well lead one to ask, 'What then is left of Nehru's socialism?' Yet Nehru declared in 1948:

> I also call myself a socialist. The fundamental principles of socialism are acceptable to me, and I want India to adopt these principles.[1]

It seems clear that the 'fundamental principles' of Nehru's revised socialism were in reality reduced to two basic propositions: (1) the socialist goal of economic and social equality is completely valid, and must be attained; and (2) the trend toward a socialist economic structure, with increasing state ownership of the means of production, is a long-range trend which is desirable and inevitable in the light of modern conditions. The second part of this chapter is concerned with the former proposition; the next chapter with the latter.

THE GOAL OF ECONOMIC DEMOCRACY

As was pointed out in Chapter III Nehru has given four distinct definitions of the word 'democracy'. Briefly, he has defined democracy in terms of individual freedom, representative government, economic and social equality, and social self-discipline. The first, second and fourth definitions represent actual functioning realities, although still in an imperfect state. One can point, for example, to the freedom of religion being exercised by individuals, or to popularly elected parliaments, or to the peaceful and orderly conduct of elections (Definitions one, two and four respectively). Democracy so defined refers to realities. Democracy defined in terms of economic and social equality, on the other hand, represents an ideal, a distant goal to be pursued.[2] Nehru has at different times used various terms to describe this goal toward which society should move. Since November 1954 he has laid great stress on 'a socialistic pattern of society'.

Nehru has always emphasized the urgent necessity for working toward economic and social democracy. In her long history India successfully evolved a stable society, but failed in one vital respect, and 'because she failed in this, she fell and remains fallen'.

No solution was found for the problem of equality. India deliberately ignored this and built up her social structure on inequality,

---

[1] Speech in Lucknow. *The Hindu*, June 25, 1948, p. 6.
[2] *Supra*, p. 61.

and we have the tragic consequences of this policy in the millions of our people who till yesterday were suppressed and had little opportunity for growth.[1]

Modern democracy faces a similar crisis. The nineteenth-century democracy included the ideal that there should be no privilege—'every person should be treated by the State as of equal social and political value'.[2] This ideal was given effect to in the political sphere by the granting of one vote to every individual, regardless of other factors. But the democratic ideal never eventuated in any considerable degree of economic equality.

The awakened masses will no longer tolerate the conditions of extreme inequality in which they have been forced to exist for centuries. This is the crisis of political democracy, and it will justify itself only if it succeeds in producing the results demanded by the masses.

If it does not, it will have to yield to some other kind of economic or social structure which we may or may not like. Ultimately, it is the results that decide the structure a country will adopt.[3]

Thus, humanitarianism and expediency alike dictate the necessity for far-reaching changes in the direction of an egalitarian society.

Examining Nehru's goal of economic democracy more closely, there emerge two basic characteristics of the ideal economic structure. It would be a society in which 'human beings had equal rights and co-operated with each other for their own and the public good'.[4] The concept of economic democracy, then, would include (1) an economic structure based on equality, in which (2) co-operative effort replaces the profit motive. These principal aspects of the ideal, as perceived by Nehru, will now be dealt with.

An economic structure based on equality. The significance of man's struggle for the material goods of life was probably not fully appreciated by Nehru in his younger years, despite his strong socialistic convictions. In 1951 he declared:

---

[1] Address to National Congress, December 1929. Nehru, *India and the World*, p. 17.
[2] Nehru, *Glimpses of World History*, p. 404.
[3] Speech in the House of the People, December 15, 1952. *Jawaharlal Nehru's Speeches, 1949–53*, p. 95.
[4] *The Hindu*, July 15, 1951, p. 6.

I have been driven almost against my will to the conclusion that material well-being is just as important in human life as anything else. High standards of living are important and we must achieve them.[1]

Nehru's own 'bourgeois' background, as he described it, enabled him to attain adulthood without ever facing the problem of personal material need. Most of his adult life was spent in the struggle for independence, in which Nehru's idealism and self-sacrifice for the cause were brought to the fore. Nehru's personal lack of concern for material things made it more difficult for him to realize their full importance, as compared with other values.

But the great economic inequalities of India, so evident on every hand, impressed Nehru deeply from the beginning, and the ultimate ideal of equality was always before him. Nehru was thinking primarily of the goal of equality when he declared in 1928, 'I do believe in communism as an ideal of society'.[2] Writing in 1933, he referred to communism as an ideal which aims at common possession and enjoyment of almost everything that the people require, thus ensuring true equality.[3] In 1939 he wrote that equality was the *sine qua non* of liberty and democracy, and this equality could not be brought about 'so long as the principal instruments of production are privately owned'.[4] In the Objectives Resolution moved by Nehru in the Constituent Assembly in 1946, the Assembly resolved to draw up a Constitution wherein would be guaranteed social, economic and political justice, and 'equality of status, of opportunity, and before the law'.[5] In 1951 Nehru declared:

After all, the whole purpose of the Constitution, as proclaimed in the Directive Principles, is to move towards what I may call a caste-less and classless society. It may not have been said precisely in that way; but that is, I take it, its purpose, and anything that perpetuates the present social and economic inequalities is bad.[6]

[1] Speech in New Delhi, March 31, 1951. *Jawaharlal Nehru's Speeches, 1949–53*, p. 565.
[2] Speech in Calcutta, September 22, 1928. *Important Speeches of Jawaharlal Nehru*, p. 66.
[3] Nehru, *Recent Essays and Writings*, pp. 135–6.
[4] Nehru, *The Unity of India*, p. 117.
[5] Speech of December 13, 1946. Nehru, *Independence and After*, p. 344.
[6] Speech in the House of the People, June 1, 1951. India, *Parliamentary Debates*, 1951, Vol. XII, Part II, col. 9831.

From the brief survey given above, it can be seen that the ideal of an economic structure based on equality has been a constant and integral part of Nehru's political thinking throughout many years. Other elements of his socialism have been modified radically, but this ideal has remained unaltered.

In recent years Nehru has often used the term 'welfare state' in describing one aspect of the goal of economic equality which India should pursue.

> This will mean our deliberately aiming at a new type of society whose chief purpose is the welfare of the people, not only in material living standards but also in the things of the spirit. This is the Welfare State....[1]

The Congress Working Committee in 1950 endorsed Nehru's resolution on the Economic Programme, which clearly set forth the Congress objective for the nation.

> That objective is the establishment of a 'Welfare State' wherein there is economic democracy, a national minimum standard in respect of the essentials of physical and social well-being, a rise in the standard of living of the people, full employment, elimination of exploitation, the progressive narrowing down of disparities in income and wealth, so that there may be equality of opportunity to all for self-development and the growth of personality.[2]

Thus Nehru considered that economic equality was just as necessary as individual freedom for the development of human personality.

Early in 1953, informal discussions were held between Nehru as Congress President and Jai Prakash Narain, leader of the Praja-Socialist Party. The object of the talks was to explore the possibility of co-operation between the two parties in certain areas of common interest and concern. The discussions and correspondence between the two leaders are of great value in delineating Nehru's beliefs about socialism. Regarding the present point—the goal of an economic structure based on equality—it is interesting to note one part of a letter from Nehru to Narain.

> You say that the goals and values of Socialism are unalterably fixed for you, and you define these goals as the creation of a new society in which there is no exploitation, in which there is economic and

[1] Nehru, *Report to the All-India Congress Committee*, 1951, p. 8.
[2] *The Hindu*, September 20, 1950, p. 4.

social equality, and in which there is freedom and well-being for all. Surely, there is hardly an intelligent person in the world who will not agree with that goal or those values. Certainly I accept them completely.[1]

Thus, the ideal of an economic structure based on equality is so widely accepted today that it can hardly be thought of as a socialistic distinctive, although it was such originally. Nehru felt that they differed on methods and procedures rather than on objectives; 'I confess that I have a feeling of groping forward step by step, even though the goal might be clear'.[2]

Co-operative effort in place of the profit motive. This is the second aspect of the goal of economic democracy as envisaged by Nehru. In the new society which was to be built up, competition would be replaced by co-operation. Just as India would have to avoid the authoritarianism of modern communist practice, so also she would have to avoid unregulated private enterprise. Nehru wrote in 1951, 'We have to try to replace the acquisitive instinct with the spirit of co-operative effort in a common cause'.[3] This means a fundamental change in society.

We have to aim deliberately at a social philosophy which seeks a fundamental transformation of this structure, at a society which is not dominated by the urge for private profit and by individual greed and in which there is fair distribution of political and economic power.[4]

The transformation would mean 'an upsetting of the present-day acquisitive society based primarily on the profit motive'.[5]

This second aspect of the goal of economic democracy, like the first, has long been a part of Nehru's political philosophy, and has remained almost unchanged up to the present time. In a letter written to an English friend in 1936, Nehru discussed the psychological problems involved in transforming individual motivation. He wrote that real socialism 'involves a profound transformation of the deeper habits of opinion and of character, and this inevitably takes time'.[6] As Nehru analyzed the problem, the main question was how to create an *environment*

---

[1] Letter to Jai Prakash Narain. *The Hindu*, March 20, 1953, p. 4.
[2] *Loc. cit.*
[3] Nehru, *Report to the All-India Congress Committee*, 1951, p. 8.
[4] Radio talk, December 31, 1952. *Jawaharlal Nehru's Speeches, 1949–53*, p. 103.
[5] Nehru, *The Discovery of India*, p. 534.
[6] Nehru, *India and the World*, pp. 179–80.

in which this deep transformation of individual character could take place.

> Under present circumstances the environment is against us, and instead of lessening our mutual hatreds and selfishness and acquisitiveness, which lead to conflict, actually encourages these evil traits.[1]

Capitalism, as a system, despite its great success in solving the problems of production, has stimulated the deeper instincts which society should now get rid of. It is impossible to progress along socialistic lines in a social and economic structure based on acquisitiveness. It is thus necessary to make a complete change-over from the capitalist system 'in order to develop new and more desirable habits and ways of thinking'.[2]

This problem was brought to the fore in Nehru's discussions with Gandhi. While Nehru's approach started with society and then proceeded to the individual, Gandhi's approach went from the individual to society—from personal to social redemption. 'Gandhi wants to improve the individual internally, morally and spiritually, and thereby to change the external environment.'[3] Nehru felt that Gandhi's approach would be futile as long as society continued to be based on acquisitiveness, for the profit motive inevitably led to conflict.

> The whole system protects and gives every scope to man's predatory instincts; it encourages some finer instincts, no doubt, but much more the baser instincts of man. Success means the knocking down of others and mounting on their vanquished selves.[4]

Nehru did not see how Gandhi could ever achieve his ideal of the moral man in such an environment. Some few individuals might respond, but the vast majority would follow the standards of the acquisitive society. Nehru also was concerned with the moral problem, but he found its roots in the social structure. In 1954 he declared: 'I consider it immoral, that is, basing your society purely on the acquisitive instinct'.[5] He felt that such a basis for society was 'absolutely out of date', and that it 'has not passed but is passing'.[6]

---

[1] *Loc. cit.*
[2] *Loc. cit.*
[3] Nehru, *Toward Freedom*, p. 320.
[4] *Ibid.*, p. 321.
[5] Speech in New Delhi. *The Hindu*, November 11, 1954, p. 5.
[6] *Loc. cit.*

Writing in 1944 Nehru expressed the view that in the future the profit motive might continue to some extent, but would not be the dominating factor in Indian society. He pointed out that 'the Indian outlook, even of the masses, has never approved of the spirit of acquisitiveness'.[1] The possessor of wealth may be envied, but respect and honour still go to the one who is capable of self-sacrifice for a higher cause. Furthermore, the co-operative effort implied in collectivism is 'fully in harmony with old Indian social conceptions, which were all based on the idea of the group'.[2] The decay of the self-governing co-operative village under British rule, according to Nehru, was largely responsible for the loss of the spirit of co-operation in Indian society. This spirit must be revived. Thus, the goal of economic democracy will be attained when society is reconstructed on the basis of two principles, equality and co-operative effort.

The chapter may be summarized here in a few paragraphs. In the late 1920s Nehru was attracted to Marxism, chiefly because of three main elements which he found in that system: a philosophy which gave meaning to the historical process, a scientific approach to the problems of society, and a moral concern for the poverty-stricken masses. Although at that time Nehru accepted the fundamentals of Marxist theory, he did not regard it as unquestionable dogma.

By 1955 Nehru had greatly modified his earlier views on three important aspects of socialist theory. He no longer felt that the world was faced with a clear-cut choice between socialism and capitalism, for these economic systems had themselves been greatly modified to meet changing conditions. Nehru believed that there was a middle way between the extremes of capitalism and collectivism. Secondly, by 1955 he had tempered his views on the class struggle. Nehru wrote that it was not by denial or non-recognition of conflicting interests that he proceeded, but that he did not want to encourage and intensify these conflicts. The best method of solving them would be through a peaceful and friendly approach. Thirdly, by 1955 Nehru asserted not only that the socialist state *could* be attained

[1] Nehru, *The Discovery of India*, p. 534.
[2] *Loc. cit.*

through the democratic process, but that this was the *only* way to build it on a firm foundation. Democratic functioning necessitated a more complicated procedure and took a longer time, but justified itself in that it gave due consideration to the individual.

Nehru continued to stress the socialist objective. This had two elements: a society based on economic and social equality, a society in which co-operative effort would replace the profit motive. The goal was a classless and a casteless society, and this was in keeping with the spirit of the present age, according to Nehru. The acquisitive instinct had been dominant in a society controlled by the profit motive; in the socialist society of the future mutual co-operation would replace individual greed.

VI

ECONOMIC DEMOCRACY: THE APPROACH

I do not mean to go in for comparisons but the old Soviet approach to planning was different from ours, both from the point of view of objectives and that of the methods adopted . . . In view of the fact that we function under a democratic setup, which we have deliberately adopted and enshrined in our Constitution and in this Parliament, any planning that we do must naturally be within that setup.

Speech in Parliament, 1952.

CHAPTER VI

ECONOMIC DEMOCRACY: THE APPROACH

THE first part of this chapter is devoted to the means by which Nehru hopes to lead India toward economic democracy; the second part to Nehru's ideas on the land problem in India, a characteristically Asian aspect of the over-all problem of economic inequality.

THE MIDDLE WAY: A MIXED ECONOMY

Nehru in 1935 was quite sure that the economic salvation of India and the world lay in a socialist setup, with most if not all of the means of production in the hands of the State. In 1955 he confessed that although the socialist ideal was still before him, he had a feeling of groping forward, step by step. But if Nehru had not evolved a clear-cut economic doctrine, he had adopted a definite approach to the problem.

The pragmatic approach. As was apointed out above, Nehru was attracted to what he regarded as the 'scientific approach' of Marxism.[1] This attraction was natural, for Nehru's attachment to the scientific method has been a life-long one, probably the only element of his life philosophy which has remained constant from his college days to the present. Nehru's admiration for Soviet Russia lay in the fact that its leaders had adopted a new spirit ('This spirit was the spirit of science') in economic development.[2] In later years Nehru's thinking underwent a gradual but profound change, and the conflict inherent in the union between Marxian theory and the scientific method came to the surface. The scientific approach indicated the need for an open mind, and a cautious trial-and-error procedure in meeting the problems of society. Marxian theory provided a ready-made analysis and solution formulated in the nineteenth century. Nehru's life-long attachment to science prevailed, and this resulted in a pragmatism which demanded of any theory just one thing: concrete results.

[1] *Supra*, pp. 102-3.
[2] Nehru, *Glimpses of World History*, p. 857.

Nehru stated that theories have a certain value—'We can use a theory for the purpose of argument and for testing its validity'.[1] But in practice one must take the facts of the situation and adapt the theory accordingly. Even Soviet Russia, which claims to base her system on a rigid theory of Marxism, re-interprets Marxism to fit changing conditions. As a consequence, 'her brand of Marxism has little to do with Marx'.[2] The Russians are hard realists and have not chained themselves to past interpretations. Theories in themselves do not indicate solutions to a specific problem, but merely mean 'a certain approach in understanding and in trying to find a solution to that problem'.[3] But no problems are solved merely by passing a law stating that the country's economy will be capitalist, or socialist, or communist. An approach is not enough; definite and precise steps have to be taken.

Theories, therefore, will justify themselves only if they are successfully used to produce results. Regarding political systems, democracy or authoritarianism will ultimately prevail in accordance with the results produced by each. The fact that one favoured democracy did not necessarily mean that it would produce the needed results. 'Ultimately,' Nehru insisted, 'it is a question of which setup and which structure of government—political or economic—pays the highest dividends.'[4] If one particular type of democracy did not produce results, it might have to be changed or even discarded for another type. The hard fact is that democracy and all it stands for might go down before authoritarianism if the latter produces superior results.

Regarding economic systems, the same test of results must be applied. Capitalism is on trial today. If it cannot solve the problem of distribution, some other way will have to be found. In modern India, if the present form of economic organization cannot be used to solve the basic problems of food, clothing and housing for the masses, it will be swept away, regardless of the ideological label of the government.

[1] Speech in New Delhi, December 26, 1950. *Jawaharlal Nehru's Speeches, 1949–53*, p. 17.
[2] *Loc. cit.*
[3] India, *Parliamentary Debates*, 1951, Vol. IX, Part II, col. 4541.
[4] Speech in the House of the People, February 18, 1953. *Jawaharlal Nehru's Speeches, 1949–53*, p. 252.

So ultimately these major problems of the day are not going to be solved by argument or by war but by the method that succeeds in delivering the goods. Whatever the method may be, the method which delivers the goods and brings about the necessary changes and gives satisfaction to the masses will justify itself and give hope.[1]

In the present world situation, 'no amount of theorizing and no amount of warfare can make the system that does not deliver the goods survive'.[2]

The recognition of two facts, (1) the limitations of economic theories as such, and (2) the urgent need for practical, tangible results, is at the base of Nehru's pragmatic approach. Referring to capitalism, socialism, etc., he declared:

I am not enamoured of these 'isms' and my approach is, and I should like to say the country's approach should be, rather a pragmatic approach in considering the problem and I want to forget the 'ism' attached to it.[3]

He was interested in seeing the people of India started on the road of progress, and 'I do not care what 'ism' it is that helps me to set them on that road', and furthermore, 'if one thing fails, we will try another'.[4] In describing the Government's Five Year Plan, Nehru said, 'The plan is not based on any dogmatic or doctrinaire approach to our problems; nor is it rigid . . . As we learn from experience we shall improve it'.[5] On another occasion he declared, 'The method of working out a plan is ultimately the method of trial and error'.[6] Chester Bowles, former United States Ambassador to India, gave this analysis of Nehru's economic policy:

He always seemed to me to be a thorough pragmatist on the question of economic development. He has announced himself in favour of private ownership wherever it will work, government ownership where that will work, and the use of co-operatives in other fields.[7]

The pragmatic approach lacked the intellectual attractiveness of Nehru's earlier socialistic ideas, but it promised to

[1] Speech in New Delhi, March 4, 1949. Nehru, *Independence and After*, p. 190.
[2] Speech of May 16, 1949. India, *Constituent Assembly Debates*, Vol. VIII, p. 7.
[3] Speech in New Delhi, March 4, 1949. Nehru, *Independence and After*, p. 190.
[4] *Ibid.*, p. 191.
[5] Radio talk, December 31, 1952. *Jawaharlal Nehru's Speeches, 1949-53*, p. 105.
[6] Speech in the House of the People, December 15, 1952. *Ibid.*, p. 98.
[7] Bowles, *Ambassador's Report*, p. 106.

produce the results so desperately desired. In order to attain
these results, certain priorities would have to be determined.

Production the first essential. Between Nehru's ultimate goal of
economic democracy and present conditions there must be
many intermediate goals, the most important of which is greatly
increased production. Nehru pointed out that most of the economic ideologies are mainly concerned with the question of
distribution of the wealth produced. These ideologies arose in
the industrialized countries of the West, in which the problem
of production had largely been solved. But the question of production must be given first place in an underdeveloped country
like India, for 'there must obviously be something substantial
to distribute before we can start the process of distribution'.[1]
At the present time, about the only thing that could be distributed is poverty. The most pressing need is that India's national
wealth be greatly increased; her industrial and agricultural
output must gradually approach that of Europe and America.
Nehru did not suggest that the entire problem of distribution
be shelved until the desired increase of production should be
attained. The two questions are intimately related. Nehru
declared in 1947:

> We may here and there make some adjustment by a more equitable
> distribution of the existing wealth. That must be done really not so
> much because it makes too much of a difference in raising the
> standard of life—it does, but not very much—but it must be done
> because it creates conditions for advance.[2]

The beneficial results would be more psychological than material. Of course, where there are gross inequalities, these should
be rapidly reduced. But in the long run, 'more wealth can only
come from more production of all types and kinds of goods'.[3]

Economic policy, then, must be hammered out on the basis
of this primary consideration: how will production be affected?
Nehru asserted, 'I am prepared to say that everything that we
do should be judged from the point of view of production first
of all'.[4] If nationalization of all the existing industries would

[1] Speech in New Delhi, December 18, 1947. Nehru, *Independence and After*,
p. 148.
[2] *Ibid.*, p. 150.
[3] *Ibid.*, p. 151.
[4] Speech in the Constituent Assembly (Legislative), January 17, 1948. *Ibid.*,
p. 164.

increase production, this would be the course to follow. But there is no reason to believe that nationalization would necessarily mean greater production. The industrial structure of the country would remain the same, except that ownership would be transferred from private hands to the State's hands. But the industrial output would probably be no greater. The State would thus rapidly expend its limited financial resources paying compensation, without increasing national productivity. Therefore, it would be far better to leave existing industries basically as they are, and use all the available financial resources of the State for starting new industries—State-owned or partially State-owned—which would definitely increase production.[1]

Some had urged that the Government nationalize the existing industries without compensation, that is, by expropriation. While Nehru pointed out that such action was quite opposed to the principles of the Constitution, he added that he did not have 'extreme moral scruples' about the matter. It was not morality but a practical consideration which militated against such a course of action. Expropriation would produce new problems and conflicts, and the confusion thus created would certainly result in the lowering of production.[2] This consideration was undoubtedly the most important in determining the role of foreign capital in India. Regarding existing foreign interests Nehru stated in Parliament that 'Government do not intend to place any restriction or impose any conditions which are not applicable to similar Indian enterprise'.[3] Production should not be interfered with.

A mixed economy. Nehru's pragmatic approach to India's economic problems led him to regard production as the first essential. It also led him to the conviction that a flexible mixed economy was the best economic structure for present-day India.

The concept of a mixed economy is a simple one, involving the recognition of two main divisions in the country's economy —the public sector and the private sector. The public sector would include all the State-owned and State-controlled industries. Eventually all of the basic heavy industries and those

[1] *The Hindu*, August 6, 1949, p. 4.
[2] *The Hindu*, October 10, 1952, p. 8.
[3] *The Hindu*, April 7, 1949, p. 4.

most vitally connected with defence production should come within the public sector. The private sector would include everything remaining under private ownership, which would be considerable. Agriculture, which is still the base of India's economy, would remain almost entirely in the private sector. Thus a large field for private enterprise would continue.

The private sector, however, must also be a controlled sector, to some extent, in that it must accept the objectives of the national plan and fit into it. In explaining the report of the Planning Commission to Parliament Nehru declared:

> The control over the private sector will relate not only to its dividends and profits but will extend to all the strategic points in the economy of the country.[1]

Nehru envisages increasing control over the private sector as time goes on, and also the widening of the public sector when conditions warrant it. In the Congress draft Election Manifesto proposed by Nehru in 1951 it is stated:

> The progressive extension of the public sector in the field of what is now the private sector must depend on various factors, including the results achieved, the resources available and the capacity of the country at the moment. The test should always be what serves the social ends in view.[2]

Thus, India's mixed economy must be flexible, and capable of being adapted to changing conditions.

The reasoning behind the idea of a mixed economy is as follows. Theoretically, the choice in economic systems is between some kind of capitalism and some kind of collectivism. Both have obvious weaknesses. The old style capitalism is a thing of the past. Nehru remarked that the doctrine of *laissez-faire* is 'almost as dead as the century which produced it — dead even in the countries where people talk about it most'.[3] The ideas of free enterprise and an absolutely free market have become out of date, because 'an economy based on them soon becomes unmanageable'.[4]

[1] Speech in the House of the People, December 15, 1952. *Jawaharlal Nehru's Speeches, 1949–53*, p. 98.
[2] *The Hindu*, July 14, 1951, p. 6.
[3] Speech in the House of the People, December 15, 1952. *Jawaharlal Nehru's Speeches, 1949–53*, p. 100.
[4] Speech in the House of the People, November 18, 1952. *Jawaharlal Nehru's Speeches, 1949–53*, p. 76.

Inevitably, therefore, the world moves toward some kind of collectivism.

In fact, not because you think or I think or anybody thinks so, inevitably the trend of events is to make the State more and more the organizer of constructive industry, and not the private capitalist or any one else. This is quite inevitable as far as I can see objectively.[1]

Extreme collectivism, however, produces certain dangers, for 'there is an obvious tendency in too much collectivism for democracy to go by the board'.[2] In over-collectivization, free thought and individual initiative are sacrificed to the system. Where human creativity is thus stifled, the inner decay of a people or a civilization must surely follow. Democracy and individual freedom are absolutely essential. 'Therefore, if one values that background of democracy, one wants to retain it and as a result you get what is called a mixed economy.'[3] The best course does not lie toward the extreme right or left; there is a middle way.

Nehru has often expressed the belief that it would be foolish for India to attempt to copy blindly the economic structure of other countries, even though they have been successful. The United States of America is an economically powerful and highly industrialized country, but

Are we to introduce their methods and techniques in our underdeveloped economy, or are we to copy the Russian methods regardless of their applicability here?[4]

The policy of a mixed economy enabled the Government of India to start building upon the existing economic structure without subjecting it to a sudden and complete upset. There is a continuity along with the necessary changes and improvements.

Opinions may differ as to what is to be done and how. But once the fundamental factor of continuity and change on the basis of continuity is accepted the difference of opinion is not vital.[5]

[1] Speech in the Constituent Assembly (Legislative), April 7, 1948. Nehru, *Independence and After*, p. 175.
[2] Speech in New Delhi. *The Hindu*, March 8, 1953, p. 7.
[3] *Loc. cit.*
[4] Speech of January 23, 1954. *Presidential Address to the Indian National Congress*, p. 17.
[5] *The Hindu*, January 25, 1949, p. 4.

A mixed economy provides for such change on the basis of continuity.

Commenting on the report of the Planning Commission, Nehru mentioned the limiting factors within which the Commission had to proceed. One of these factors was that it had to accept the present economic structure of the country.

> It proceeded on the basis of changing it with as much speed as might be possible, but nevertheless accepting things as they are and gradually changing them in a particular direction.[1]

Nobody wants the *status quo* to continue, nevertheless the Commission could not proceed on the basis of sweeping it away overnight. In other words, planning would have to proceed along the lines of the evolutionary socialism, reformism, or gradualism about which Nehru had such grave doubts twenty years earlier. But it suited Indian conditions of the present, for the country could not stand further disruption and strife.

Considering both the private sector and the public sector, Nehru found a mixed economy peculiarly suited to India's economic situation. The less vital industries will remain in the private sector, and this is advantageous for the country's economic development. For the socialization of all industry would mean a huge outlay of money in compensation by the Government, which it could not afford with its present limited resources. If the State did undertake to nationalize these industries, this would still not result in increased production, which is the most important immediate goal. Furthermore, the money thus spent would be diverted from the large new projects which have been started within the public sector, and which in time will greatly add to production.

> But it seems to me a far better approach to the problem for the State to concentrate more and more on new industries of the latest type and to control them in a large measure, because then the resources of the State go towards further progress and controlled progress instead of merely trying to get hold of something which exists.[2]

The private sector is thus indispensable at India's present point of development. Nehru also suggested that the private sector

---

[1] Speech in the House of the People, October 15, 1951. India, *Parliamentary Debates*, 1951, Vol. XVI, Part II, col. 5044.

[2] Speech in New Delhi, December 18, 1947. Nehru, *Independence and After*, p. 154.

could incidentally perform a valuable function in helping to keep the public sector up to the mark. If the public sector were to have the field unchallenged, it would tend to grow careless. However, 'the existence of state enterprise side by side with private enterprise may also prove healthy in the present circumstances as providing some kind of competition between the two'.[1]

A point which Nehru has repeatedly made is that the problem must not be approached on the basis of a static technology. Socialists and communists base their programmes on a more or less static world, without taking into account the new methods and techniques of production which are being developed. They urge the State to acquire the existing industrial apparatus, which may be ninety percent obsolete in view of present technological advances. In modern India, a mixed economy is the most practical policy, for the limited resources of the State need not be spent in socializing industries based on an outdated technology. These can be allowed to remain in the private sector. Rather, the State can turn its attention and resources to the new techniques, and new sources of power which are being tapped, such as atomic energy. From this discussion it can be seen that in Nehru's opinion, the private sector performs a definite and important function in this transitional period of the Indian economy, and could not be dispensed with.

Likewise, the public sector is indispensable in meeting the requirements of present-day conditions in India. The most important reason, Nehru asserted, is that Indian private capital and industry are clearly not sufficiently developed to undertake the huge projects which must be carried out. Private enterprise in America developed gradually and built up a very strong position for itself, with large resources. Private enterprise in India has simply not reached that point. Nehru posed the question:

Is our private enterprise going to take up our river valley schemes? It cannot, because they are too big for it. These schemes cannot pay dividends quickly. We have to wait for years and years. Therefore, the State inevitably has to take them up.[2]

The State alone has the financial resources for such projects.

[1] Nehru, *Report to the All-India Congress Committee*, 1955, p. 11.
[2] Speech in New Delhi, December 26, 1950. *Jawaharlal Nehru's Speeches, 1949–53*, p. 19.

Then too, certain industries such as defence and atomic energy
are so vital to the State's security that they also must be the
exclusive monopoly of the State. Nehru declared in 1954 that:

> ..we found that no State can allow atomic energy to be deve-
> loped in a private way—it is much too dangerous a thing for a
> private agency to develop.[1]

Therefore, leaving aside all questions of economic ideologies,
the public sector in India's economy is absolutely indispensable
for several very practical reasons, according to Nehru's view.

In a mixed economy there is a real place for the cottage and
village industries which Gandhi did so much to encourage.
Nehru pointed out that during the nationalist struggle, *khadi*
(hand-spun and woven cloth) became a revolutionary symbol
which far outweighed its economic value. Today cottage industries could only be developed on the basis of their economic
contribution. They are not an alternative to large-scale industrialization, for this must ultimately come, and the sooner the
better. But Nehru views village industries as having a com-
plementary function, and as being useful in providing employment and adding to production. The cost of employing one
man in heavy industry is very high, approximately 10,000
rupees. It is clear that the public and private sectors combined
could not at present solve the unemployment problem on the
basis of costly industrialization. Therefore, cottage and village
industries, remaining within the private sector, can make a
valuable contribution in helping to provide employment.

A mixed economy is the middle way which is well suited to
present Indian conditions, and which promises to produce results. The public sector plays an indispensable role, but no less
important is that of the private sector in this period of transition.
Nehru pointed out that in some industries the two sectors meet,
where the State had acquired a fifty percent share of the total
capital.[2] The great advantage of a mixed economy was its flexibility and capacity for adaptation to changing conditions.

The basic framework of a mixed economy was envisaged in
a resolution drafted by the Government less than a year after
independence. The Resolution on Industrial Policy, presented
to Parliament on April 6, 1948, recognized three categories of

[1] Speech in New Delhi. *The Hindu*, November 28, 1954, p. 7.
[2] *The Hindu*, December 6, 1949, p. 11.

industries. The first category, referring to the public sector, has two sub-divisions. (1) The manufacture of arms and ammunition, the production and control of atomic energy, and the ownership and management of railways transport should be the *exclusive monopoly* of the Central Government. (2) In such industries as coal, iron and steel, aircraft manufacture, shipbuilding, etc., the State (here meaning State Governments as well as the Central Government) should be *exclusively responsible* for the establishment of *new* undertakings. Existing private undertakings in these fields would be allowed to continue to develop, and the question of their future would be reviewed after a period of ten years.

The second category is the private sector, and those industries not included in the first category would normally be open to private enterprise, individual as well as co-operative. The State would also progressively participate in this field, and had already begun large multi-purpose river-valley projects, the production of fertilizer, etc. The third category includes certain basic industries the location of which must be governed by economic factors of national importance, or which require a high degree of technical skill. These industries will be the subject of central regulation and control, and include salt, automobiles and tractors, machine tools, heavy chemicals, etc. In these fields, special planning and regulation by the Central Government is necessary in the national interest.[1]

A socialistic pattern of society. In November 1954 Nehru, in an address to the National Development Council, declared that they had arrived at a new stage in their planning, especially in relation to the second Five-Year Plan. The time had come for a further clarification of the objectives of national planning in India. Nehru envisaged a 'socialistic pattern of society' as the goal at which they were aiming. He used the term, not in a dogmatic sense, but 'in the sense of meaning largely that the means of production should be socially owned and controlled for the benefit of society as a whole'.[2] He had no intention of doing away with private enterprise, however. There was still much scope for it, and it should be given freedom and encouragement to develop.

[1] *The Hindu*, April 7, 1948, p. 4.
[2] *The Hindu*, November 11, 1954, p. 5.

As Nehru continued to stress the aim of a socialistic pattern of society, there was considerable speculation that a radical departure from existing policy was about to be made. Nehru explained, however, that there was to be no basic change in the policy of a mixed economy, as set forth in the Industrial Policy Resolution of 1948. There would be a shift of emphasis in favour of more and more State ownership and control of new industries.[1] It was inevitable that in an expanding economy in an underdeveloped country with limited resources, the public sector would grow steadily.[2] But private enterprise would continue to have a large field in which to operate.

At the conclusion of the December 1954 debate in the House of the People on economic policy, the House passed the following resolution.

> This House having considered the economic situation in India and the policy of the Government in relation thereto is of the opinion that (1) the policy of the Government is in harmony with the policy statement of 6th April, 1948, (2) the objective of our economic policy should be a socialist pattern of society and (3) towards this end the tempo of economic activity in general and industrial development in particular should be stepped up to the maximum extent possible.[3]

The Indian National Congress, meeting at Avadi in January 1955, unanimously passed a resolution pledging the Congress to the establishment of a socialistic pattern of society. The resolution, which was moved by Nehru in the plenary session, specified that in such a society 'the principal means of production are under social ownership or control, production is progressively speeded up and there is equitable distribution of the national wealth'.[4]

Nehru emphasized that this was by no means a new departure from the Congress objective of establishing 'a co-operative commonwealth based on equality of opportunity and of political, economic and social rights'.[5] The new resolution 'clarifies this idea and draws the attention of the people to it

---

[1] *The Hindu*, December 7, 1954, p. 4. *Supra.*, pp. 108, 125.
[2] *The Hindu*, December 22, 1954, p. 4.
[3] *The Hindu*, December 23, 1954, p. 5.
[4] *The Hindu*, January 20, 1955, p. 5, and January 23, 1955, p. 5.
[5] *The Hindu*, January 18, 1955, p. 8. The quotation is from Article 1 of the Congress Constitution.

in a more forceful manner'.[1] It appears that the new phrase was intended more as an educational device than anything else.

Nehru denied charges that the Congress was merely raising a new slogan. However, it is interesting to recall that in 1948 Nehru opposed Kazi Syed Karimuddin's resolution in the Constituent Assembly which stated: 'This Assembly is of the opinion that the economic pattern of this country shall be a socialist economy . . .'[2] Nehru asserted that the resolution was vague and had little meaning except to show the goodness of heart of the Honourable Member. It is difficult to see how the Avadi Congress resolution could escape the same criticism. At any rate, it appears unlikely that any radical changes in economic policy will be effected because of this resolution, at least in the near future. The basic structure of a mixed economy will probably continue in India for some years to come.

THE PROBLEM OF LAND

In this section, Nehru's views on a peculiarly Asian problem are considered. Nehru is indebted to Europe for most of the ideas on economics which he has adopted at various stages of his life. The problem of land is one to which nineteenth century European socialistic thought had not addressed itself to any great extent.

Landlordism in India. As pointed out in *The Discovery of India*, the present land system is of relatively recent origin in India. The following is Nehru's description of its development. Prior to the advent of the British, there was nothing comparable to the European feudal system in which the land belonged to the feudal lord and ultimately, through him, to the king. The king, in India, collected taxes from the land and often delegated this revenue-collecting authority to others, but the peasant was not the lord's serf. Each village was a more or less self-contained unit based on the co-operation of the individual peasants. The individual farmer did not 'own' the patch of land he worked; rather, there was a conception of communal ownership, 'not so much of the land as of the produce of the land'.[3]

[1] *The Hindu*, January 23, 1955, p. 5.

[2] Speech in the Constituent Assembly (Legislative), February 17, 1948. Nehru, *Independence and After*, p. 163.

[3] Nehru, *The Discovery of India*, p. 303.

9

Thus in India there was no landlord system, as known in the West, nor was the individual peasant the full owner of his patch of land. Both these concepts were introduced much later by the British with disastrous results.[1]

The landlord system was but another undesirable product of imperialism in India.

The British governors, who themselves represented the English landed class, introduced something similar to the English land system in Bengal and Bihar. At first they appointed revenue-farmers, *zamindars*, charged with collecting the land tax and paying it to the government. In time they developed into virtual landlords.

The village community was deprived of all control over the land and its produce; what had always been considered as the chief interest and concern of that community now became the private property of the newly created landowner.[2]

The corporate character of the village unit and the co-operative basis of community life broke down, and the new landlord-tenant relationship became the most important one. The British introduced different forms of land ownership in different regions, but many big landowners emerged from the process. Nehru asserted that this was a deliberate policy of the British, whereby a new class was created whose interests depended upon the continuance of British rule.[3]

Regardless of its origin, almost all agree that the problem of landlordism is a most serious one in modern India. In its extreme form, the landless tenant's share of his crop is so small that he can scarcely eke out a bare subsistence. In 1952, in the Tanjore district of Madras state, the farmers were paying 75 or 80 percent of their crop to the owner, and the expenses of the next crop had to come from the remainder. In that district three-fourths of the farmers were leasing or working land owned by others. Of the one-fourth who were landowners, three percent owned 50 percent of the land. The situation in the district has improved somewhat since 1952, but still remains bad.[4] While this is an extreme example, it is representative of the type

[1] *Ibid.*, p. 246.
[2] *Ibid.*, p. 303.
[3] *Ibid.*, p. 304.
[4] Bowles, *Ambassador's Report*, p. 174.

of land problem found in many parts of India. One expert reported that the land inequalities in parts of India were 'as bad or even worse than he had seen anywhere else in Asia'.[1]

Nehru's experience with the peasants of Oudh in 1920 was described by him as a turning-point in his life, and has already been referred to.[2] From that time on he became increasingly concerned over the problems of land reform. Of the pre-1935 period he wrote, 'For the Congress the agrarian question was the dominating social issue, and much time had been given to its study and the formulation of policy'.[3] Nehru drafted the 1936 Lucknow Congress resolution on Agarian Programme, which stated in part:

> This Congress is of the opinion that the most important and urgent problem of the country is the appalling poverty, unemployment and indebtedness of the peasantry, fundamentally due to antiquated and repressive land tenure and revenue systems,....[4]

The resolution went on to declare that the final solution of the problem could not be found until British imperialism withdrew from India, after which the land system could be thoroughly changed.

Land reform was apparently a subject on which Nehru's convictions came into conflict with Gandhi's. Gandhi stated that he was 'never in favour of abolition of the *talukdari* or *zamindari* system'.[5] His objective was to reach the hearts of the big landlords and convert them, so that they would hold their land in trust for their tenants, for whose welfare it would be used. Nehru, on the other hand, considered that 'this semi-feudal system is out of date and is a great hindrance to production and general progress'.[6]

As early as 1928, Nehru expressed definite views as to precisely how the *zamindari* problem should be dealt with. Addressing the United Provinces Congress Conference, Nehru asserted that the size of land holdings should be limited by law to what was ordinarily enough for a family to cultivate. Furthermore, 'in

---

[1] Statement of Wolf Ladejinsky. *Ibid.*, p. 185.
[2] *Supra*, pp. 14, 39.
[3] Nehru, *The Discovery of India*, p. 375.
[4] Nehru, *The Unity of India*, p. 408.
[5] Nehru, *Toward Freedom*, p. 325.
[6] *Loc. cit.*

order to prevent accumulations, we must prohibit all alienations of land and all transfers for debt'.[1]

Raising the question as to the basis on which the big estates should be abolished, Nehru considered the relative merits of confiscation and full compensation. The latter would be patently impossible, since the State did not have the enormous amount of money which it would require. The only way to get the money would be by a great burden of taxation on the land in which case the peasant holder would be no better off than when he was a tenant. In the case of full compensation,

> The only person who will profit will be the *zamindar* who will be saved all trouble and worry and will get hard cash instead of a varying and troublesome income.[2]

If this plan were followed, there would be no attempt at equalization of wealth. For these reasons Nehru rejected the possibility of full compensation. Confiscation, on the other hand, would lead to many cases of hardship, which should also be avoided. Nehru therefore advocated the middle way involving limited compensation, but warned that 'compensation should certainly not be given so as to make the receiver of it a wealthy man again'.[3]

Upon the attainment of independence, Nehru and the Congress were called upon to make good their past pledges. Nehru was fully aware of the seriousness of the matter.

> Now this whole concept of the abolition of the *zamindari* system came up before us, because we felt this inner urge of our people, because we heard the cry of millions of people and sometimes those deep murmurs and rumblings, which if not listened to and if not answered create big revolutions and changes in the country.[4]

This is the problem, Nehru asserted, which upsets constitutions and creates the big upheavals taking place throughout most of Asia today. As Nehru surveyed the forces which were moving that vast continent, he came to the conclusion that 'nothing is more important and vital than a gradual abolition of the big estates'.[5]

[1] Speech in Jhansi, October 27, 1928. *Important Speeches of Jawaharlal Nehru*, p. 125.

[2] *Loc. cit.*

[3] *Loc. cit.*

[4] Speech in the House of the People, June 1, 1951. India, *Parliamentary Debates*, 1951, Vol. XII, Part II, col. 9917.

[5] Speech in the Constituent Assembly, September 10, 1949. *Jawaharlal Nehru's Speeches, 1949–53*, p. 484.

Dynamic forces versus static rights. On September 10, 1949, Nehru proposed an article of the Draft Constitution, which was then being considered by the Constituent Assembly. This became Article 31 of the Constitution as finally adopted, and relates to the question of compensation for compulsory acquisition of property. The first clause of the article lays down the basic principle that 'no person shall be deprived of his property save by authority of law'.[1] The second clause states that the law should provide for compensation for the property acquired and should either fix the amount of the compensation or specify the principles on which it is to be determined.

Other clauses of the Article provide that bills involving compulsory acquisition of property which have been passed by the legislature of any State, and have received the President's assent, or such bills that shall have been passed and assented to at the commencement of the Constitution, should not be called in question in any court on the ground that they contravene the provisions of clause (2).[2] The article thus combines the principle of no deprivation of property except by authority of law, with provisions for the compulsory State acquisition of property upon *less than full compensation* for the same. The Article was intended to clear the way for extensive land reforms by the various State Governments.

Here it may be noted parenthetically that the Indian Constitution places responsibility for land legislation squarely on the States, and not on the Central Government. The Seventh Schedule of the Constitution is composed of three comprehensive lists of subjects regarding which power to legislate is granted to the Union Government, to the State Governments, and to both (the Concurrent List), respectively. Number 18 in the State List is as follows:

Land, that is to say, rights in or over land, land tenures including the relation of landlord and tenant, and the collection of rents; transfer and alienation of agricultural land; land improvement and agricultural loans; colonization.

Because of the widely differing land systems existing in the various States, it was believed that each State could best solve its own problem of land inequalities.

[1] *The Constitution of India,* Article 31 (1).
[2] Article 31, clauses (6) and (4) respectively.

Nehru defended the draft Article by explaining it in terms of a just compromise between the individual's right to property and the community's right to property. If the State wants to take the property, every step should be taken to ensure the individual's receiving fair and equitable compensation. But it is too often forgotten that equity applies not only to the individual but also to the community.

No individual can ultimately override the rights of the community at large. No community should injure and invade the rights of the individual, unless it be for the most urgent and important of reasons.[1]

How can the individual's right and the community's right be determined, when a specific question of land reform arises? There is no simple formula which can everywhere be applied. Rather, it is a question of *balance*, and this balance can be arrived at only by the legislature, which represents the will of the entire community.

Nehru deprecated the tendency of the judiciary to function as a kind of third house, often undoing the efforts of the legislature.

..ultimately the fact remains that the legislature must be supreme and must not be interfered with by the courts of law in measures of social reform.[2]

As Nehru pointed out on another occasion, law by its very nature was a growth by precedent. Precedent always offered society something from which it could learn, but in a dynamic situation precedent 'might also prevent that adaptation of law to the changing society which was necessary in order not to have a break or conflict'.[3]

Nehru reiterated the urgency of the social and economic problems facing the country. Land reform legislation which would affect millions of people and on which the stability of the State might depend could not be left to the time-consuming, continuous litigation in the courts of law.[4] The land question in India today was one of revolutionary implications, and could not be considered from a narrow legalistic and juristic point of

---

[1] Speech in the Constituent Assembly, September 10, 1949. *Jawaharlal Nehru's Speeches, 1949–53*, p. 480.
[2] *Ibid.*, p. 485.
[3] Speech in New Delhi. *The Hindu*, April 1, 1951, p.
[4] Speech in the Constituent Assembly, September 10, 1949. *Jawaharlal Nehru's Speeches, 1949–53*, p. 480.

view. If the envisaged solution of partial compensation were not considered just by the *zamindars*, it was still a more just way than any that might come later, for 'the latter way may not be one of legislation'.[1]

Nehru argued that the question of extensive land reform could not be considered on the same plane as the acquisition of relatively small properties for the improvement of a city. The law has been clearly laid down in regard to compensation in such cases.

> But today the community has to deal more and more with large schemes of social reform, social engineering, etc., which can hardly be considered from the point of view of individual acquisition of a small piece of land or a small structure.[2]

Restricting the State to a basis of market value compensation in these larger plans of social reform would be tantamount to ensuring the continuance of the *status quo*, for the State would never have the financial resources to carry through these plans.

Arguments against the abolition of landlordism were usually based on a certain static conception of property, as if the ownership of property were a right which had existed unchanged throughout the ages. On the contrary, Nehru asserted, 'it has changed very greatly and, even today, is undergoing a very rapid change'.[3] The concept of property at one time included human beings as slaves. Gradually slavery was abolished, and the idea of property underwent changes as human society developed.

> If you go back to the period of the great debates on slavery, you will find how the same arguments were advanced with regard to human beings as are sometimes advanced now with regard to the other forms of property.[4]

Land is still an important form of property, but in highly industrialized countries property may consist mainly of a bundle of papers—securities, promissory notes, etc., which represent millions. Increasingly, the man with credit is the real owner of property, and can do almost anything with sufficient credit. Thus, when considering the right of property,

[1] *Ibid.*, p. 484.
[2] *Ibid.*, p. 479.
[3] *Ibid.*, p. 482.
[4] *Loc. cit.*

to imagine that the present stage or yesterday's stage is static is as wrong as to imagine that the age when human beings were considered as property was right. It is a changing concept.[1]

As society thinks more and more of property in terms of the rights of the community, it becomes increasingly doubtful that the landlord has any moral right to perpetuate the relationship of extreme inequality with his tenants, regardless of legalistic arguments.

The entire object of Article 31 of the Constitution, in the form proposed by Nehru in the Constituent Assembly, was 'to take away the question of *zamindari* and land reform from the purview of the Courts'.[2] Clauses 4 and 6 specifically excluded certain land reform legislation from the jurisdiction of the courts. Nevertheless, by 1951 the Bihar High Court had obstructed similar land legislation on the basis of Article 14: 'The State shall not deny to any person equality before the law or the equal protection of the laws within the territory of India'.

This ruling was the occasion for two additions to the Constitution (Article 31 A and 31 B) in the Constitution (First Amendment) Act of 1951. The amendment was simply another attempt to save land reform legislation from judicial obstruction. 31 A stated in part:

.... no law providing for the acquisition by the State of any estate or of any rights therein ...... shall be deemed to be void on the ground that it is inconsistent with, or takes away or abridges any of the rights conferred by, any provisions of this Part.

The latter reference was to Part III, Fundamental Rights, in which the above-mentioned Article 14 appears. As Nehru pointed out in the parliamentary debate, this amendment was meant to give effect to the Constitution; it would not change the Constitution, but would make it stronger and more explicit. The amendment would grant a certain power to the State Governments to go ahead with the laws they had already passed in accordance with the Constitution.

In several speeches defending the proposed amendments, Nehru recalled that the abolition of the *zamindari* system and

---

[1] Speech in the House of the People, June 1, 1951. India, *Parliamentary Debates*, 1951, Vol. XII, Part II, col. 9921..

[2] Speech in the House of the People,, May 18, 1951. *Jawaharlal Nehru's Speeches, 1949–53*, p. 511.

agrarian reform were vital changes to which the Congress had been committed for a generation. He reiterated the urgency of the question, and declared that today 'the basic and primary problem in Asia is the land problem'.[1] In some Asian countries the problem had been dealt with quickly by absolute expropriation. Regardless of the justice or injustice of it, a new stability has been produced. India had adopted another approach, and was proceeding slowly and gradually, 'so that there is less of injustice and upset than what you will find in any country that has dealt with this problem'.[2]

Nevertheless, the new stability created by the revolutionary changes in other countries was of fundamental importance. The *zamindars* in India should realize that their security ultimately lies in a stable economic and social system, and not in legal procedures or law courts. Unless there is peace between the landlords and the vast peasant population, the former can have no security. Referring to the *zamindari* system, Nehru declared:

> That system cannot continue; it does not matter what your Fundamental Rights might say, what your Constitution might say or what your courts might say. If you refuse to see beyond these you will arrive at a revolutionary situation which will ignore all these things.[3]

India had to face these realities and adjust to them while there was still time. But progress in land reform was being held up in the courts. In the past three years some very important measures passed by various State legislatures had met this fate.

> No doubt, as I said, the interpretation of the courts must be accepted as right but in the meantime you, and I and the country have to face social and economic upheavals. How are we to meet this challenge of the times?[4]

The challenge was one of stern realities which could not be dispelled by legalistic argumentation.

The Bihar High Court had used the principle of 'equal protection of the laws' (Article 14) in declaring certain land reform laws void. The equality of law, Nehru declared, has

[1] Speech in the House of the People, May 16, 1951. *Ibid.*, p. 500.

[2] Speech in the House of the People, June 1, 1951. India, *Parliamentary Debates*, 1951, Vol. XII, Part II, col. 9918.

[3] Speech in the House of the People, May 29, 1951. *Jawaharlal Nehru's Speeches, 1949-53*, p. 532.

[4] Speech in the House of the People, May 16, 1951. *Ibid.*, p. 500.

thus come to mean 'the making of existing inequalities rigid by law'.[1] If an article in the Constitution relating to non-discrimination or equality leads one to the belief that so much compensation should be given for land compulsorily acquired, it may be perfectly correct. But, if one is also thereby led to the conclusion that this principle must be applied in such a way that it makes any major agrarian reform impossible, then obviously that article in the Constitution is wrong and must be amended. For the rights of the individual are not the only rights to be considered. They must be balanced with the rights of the community which in the final analysis are more important, for 'ultimately they affect the rights of the individual too'.[2]

The real difficulty which has to be faced, Nehru asserted, is a conflict between the dynamic ideas contained in the Directive Principles of State Policy and the static ideas contained in the Fundamental Rights of the Constitution. The Directive Principles point out the way India must travel, and represent a dynamic move toward certain objectives. Article 39(b), for example, says:

> The State shall, in particular, direct its policy towards securing—that the ownership and control of the material resources of the community are so distributed as best to subserve the common good.

The Directive Principles, with the idea of a dynamic movement toward definite goals, necessarily mean changes. The Fundamental Rights, on the other hand, 'represent something static; their object is to preserve certain rights which already exist'.[3]

In the process of dynamic movement toward certain objectives, existing static relationships are necessarily affected.

> In fact, it is meant to affect those settled relationships, and yet if you come back to the Fundamental Rights they are meant to preserve, though not always directly, certain settled relationships.[4]

Thus there is a certain conflict between the two parts of the Constitution, and the courts always lay more stress on the Fundamental Rights than on the Directive Principles. This is almost inevitable since law is basically a growth of precedent,

[1] Speech in the House of the People, May 18, 1951. *Ibid.*, p. 512.

[2] Speech in the House of the People, June 1, 1951. India, *Parliamentary Debates*, 1951, Vol. XII, Part II, col. 9918.

[3] Speech in the House of the People, May 16, 1951. *Jawaharlal Nehru's Speeches*, *1949–53*, p. 492.

[4] *Loc. cit.*

and naturally emphasizes the more static relationships. Nevertheless, the dynamic aspect of the Constitution, which was meant to lead society to something better, is hampered by this over-emphasis on the static element. Nehru saw great dangers in this situation when he declared:

> A constitution which is unchanging and static—it does not matter how good it is, how perfect it is—is a constitution that has outlived its use. It is in its old age already and gradually approaching its death. A constitution to be living must be growing, must be adaptable, must be flexible, must be changeable.[1]

These amendments, Nehru declared, were an attempt to increase this needed flexibility, while yet maintaining a basic stability.

Following the Amendment of 1951, the abolition of the big *zamindari, jagirdari* and *taluqdari* estates was largely achieved. However, the States encountered more obstruction by the courts when the next step in land reform was taken, which called forth further amendments to Articles 31 and 31A. The Statement of Objects and Reasons of the Constitution (Fourth Amendment) Bill of 1954 includes the following:

> ....our next objectives in land reform are the fixing of limits to the extent of agricultural land that may be owned or occupied by any person, the disposal of any land held in excess of the prescribed maximum and the further modification of the rights of land-owners and tenants in agricultural holdings.[2]

As finally passed, the Amendment completely removed the question of the quantum of compensation from the courts, in all cases of compulsory acquisition of either agricultural or industrial property. Nehru, using much the same arguments as before, reiterated that this amendment merely sought to clarify the original intention of the framers of the Constitution. There was no thought of the State acquiring property by expropriation. Nehru personally felt that there was no moral right attached to property, but rather than produce conflict, compensation would be given in every case. But the quantum of compensation would have to be left to the discretion of the legislatures.[3]

---

[1] Speech in the House of the People, May 29, 1951. *Ibid.*, p. 525.
[2] *The Hindu*, December 21, 1954, p. 6.
[3] *The Hindu*, December 24, 1954, p. 4.

In a preceding section, Nehru's great stress on production was discussed.[1] On one occasion he declared, 'I am prepared to say that everything that we do should be judged from the point of view of production first of all'.[2] The question arises as to how this principle applies to land reform in which large estates are divided into relatively small plots of land making scientific farming more difficult. In the debates on the 1951 amendments, one member suggested that collectivized or co-operative large-scale farming should be set up wherever land reforms are effected. Replying to this speech, Nehru stated: 'Now it is perfectly true that logically and scientifically considering, ultimately large-scale co-operative farming will be necessary'.[3] In his earlier writings Nehru also had pointed out that 'the tiny holdings, averaging a fraction of an acre per person, are uneconomic and wasteful and too small for the application of scientific methods of agriculture'.[4]

Nevertheless, to think of completely reorganizing Indian agriculture on the basis of collectivized farming at the present time was simply out of the question. Nehru cited the example of modern China working on the basis of a communist ideology. In China there are no Fundamental Rights to hold up land reform, no necessity to pay any compensation. There was a clean slate to write upon. Still, land reform in China has resulted in the creation of millions of peasant proprietors, a situation quite opposed to the communist ideal of collectivization in agriculture. Regardless of one's ideology,

> . . . . you cannot get rid of or by-pass or ignore the feelings of millions of people in your country and especially the people who are attached to the land and in whose blood there is something of that land.[5]

The deep feelings of the vast peasant population in India made land reform necessary and imperative; they also made collectivization impossible. New ideas could not be forced upon the peasant masses. They would have to be converted, and Nehru

[1] *Supra*, pp. 122-3.
[2] Speech in the Constituent Assembly (Legislative), January 17, 1948. Nehru, *Independence and After*, p. 164.
[3] Speech in the House of the People, June 1, 1951. India, *Parliamentary Debates*, 1951, Vol. XII, Part II, col. 9916.
[4] Nehru, *The Unity of India*, pp. 21-2.
[5] Speech in the House of the People, June 1, 1951. India, *Parliamentary Debates*, 1951, Vol. XII, Part II, col. 9916.

felt that the best way to do that would be by setting up model co-operative farms, living examples from which the peasants could learn.

Many who accept Nehru's goal of economic equality believe that the present approach to land reform is wrong. The critics argue that there is no logical or moral reason for the State to discriminate against those who own land, and in favour of those who own houses, factories, government bonds or bank accounts. The *zamindari* system having been abolished, the remaining land owners are mostly middle class people, who can hardly be regarded as more parasitic than factory owners.

It is claimed that the present approach results in a serious breach of the democratic principle of equal treatment of all by the State. It is in general desirable that land should be owned by the cultivators. However,

> it is but an equitable principle that any costs involved in steps toward a better or desired pattern of national economy should be proportionately borne by all wealthy sections and not shelved onto a particular section.[1]

Compulsory acquisition of land by the State for distribution to the tillers is not objected to. In these big plans of social engineering, society as a whole has a stake. But by paying the landowner considerably less than the market value of the land, he is made to bear the brunt of the changes, while wealthier sections of society remain untouched.

Another argument which is advanced is that greater equality in land holdings will not necessarily mean greater equality in living standards. The tenants who become peasant proprietors will not be very much better off in terms of housing, food, sanitation, and education. The mere transfer of ownership would produce more psychological security than real material betterment. Land reforms, in terms of the goal of true economic equality, tend to be 'spectacular but ineffective'. Steeply graded taxation would offer a surer way to the welfare state.

> The scientific administrative method for removal of inequalities is taxation of the rich to provide for the poor facilities that will help them to get even through better health, competence and education. The socialism of the Labour Party in Britain was reflected in their

[1] Rama Rao, D. V., 'Land Reform or New Untouchability?', *Swatantra*, Vol. IX, No. 31 (September 4, 1954), p. 25.

policy of making the rich pay for the uplift of the poor not through confiscatory legislation but by means of graded taxation.[1]

Landholders in India have in the past been exempt from income tax, unlike other property owners. The incomes of all should be taxed on an equal basis, regardless of the source, and the cost of raising the standard of living of the poor should be equitably distributed, according to these observers.

One aspect of the debates of land reform is that they have revealed Nehru's attitude toward the courts. He has taken a rather dim view of the role of the judiciary in the democratic system of government. The obstruction caused by the courts to *zamindari* abolition legislation was indeed disconcerting. Nevertheless, it is probable that Nehru has failed to appreciate fully the long-range value of the judiciary in the protection of the individual's rights. The United States Supreme Court decision of 1954 declaring unconstitutional racial segregation in the public schools is a notable example of the value of the process of judicial review, despite its slowness. Nehru tends to overemphasize the legislature as representing the 'sovereign will of the people', and to minimize the importance of the independent judiciary for upholding the citizen's rights.

The Fourth Amendment to the Constitution completely removes the question of the quantum of compensation for compulsorily acquired property from the jurisdiction of the courts. In the course of the debate Nehru admitted, in effect, that justiciability is a necessary adjunct of a fundamental right. The Amendment thus eliminates from the Constitution, for all practical purposes, the fundamental right of property.[2] The quantum of compensation to be given will depend wholly on the will of the legislature.

During the debate in Parliament, several Members expressed their faith in the Congress' stated policy not to resort to expropriation, but feared what might happen if a less responsible party should come to power in the future. There would be no judicial safeguards to protect the individual's property from confiscatory legislation.

According to Western democratic theory, the courts have an

---

[1] 'Socialism from the Wrong End', editorial in *Swatantra*, Vol. IX, No. 26 (July 31, 1954), p. 4.
[2] *The Hindu*, March 17, 1955, p. 4.

important function to perform—that of holding even the scales of justice between the State and the citizen. In the United States the practice of judicial review is regarded as essential to the protection of fundamental rights. Nehru probably reflected his British legal training in minimizing its importance. He dismissed the problem by merely asking, 'Is Parliament less to be trusted than the courts?' Yet the question is not one of trust but of function and position. The courts, free from the pressures of party majorities, are in a position to render justice 'because they have no vested interest in the policies which are proposed to be enforced and which might run counter to the individual's rights'.[1]

It must be concluded that Nehru's concept of the right of property is somewhat at variance with that of prevailing Western democratic thought. He has repeatedly stated that outright expropriation of land could not be considered wrong, since there was 'no moral right attached to property'.[2] The Government had adopted a policy of paying compensation chiefly because they wanted to avoid conflict. On a number of occasions Nehru has praised the 'progressive' measures of land legislation carried out in Kashmir, where all land in excess of $22\frac{3}{4}$ acres was transferred to the actual tiller without payment of any compensation at all to the owner.

As has been shown above, public opinion in India is by no means unanimously in accord with Nehru's policies on land reform. Indeed, it is not difficult to find fault with specific points in Nehru's theory. But the final evaluation must be made not in the realm of theory but in that of political realities. And in this realm the pertinent question is: has land reform under Nehru's leadership brought about a new and more equitable equilibrium in rural India without sacrificing democratic procedure? It seems clear that significant advances have been made in this direction, although much still remains to be done.

A few paragraphs may here be devoted to a summary of the chapter. Nehru's approach to the problems of India's economic development is largely a pragmatic one, in contrast to his earlier socialist ideas which tended to be somewhat doctrinaire. The

[1] Editorial in *The Hindu*, March 17, 1955, p. 4.
[2] *The Hindu*, December 24, 1954, p. 4.

ultimate socialist goal is still the same, but the means for its attainment is no longer a point of doctrine. Nehru found it necessary to determine more immediate goals, and to set priorities. He affirmed that greatly increased production of all kinds of goods was the first essential for free India, since one cannot distribute what has not been produced. A mixed economy providing a place for private enterprise (the private sector) as well as for state ownership (the public sector) seemed to offer the best prospects for immediate results. Nevertheless, Nehru regarded increased state control and ownership of industry as a long-range and inevitable trend, in India as in the rest of the world.

Nehru came into conflict with the judiciary over the question of land reform legislation. The courts were determined to protect the individual's right of property, and insisted that full compensation be paid by the State if it wanted to redistribute agricultural land. Nehru saw in this situation a conflict between the dynamic forces moving toward economic equality and the static rights of the individual. He held that in the final analysis these rights would be secure only if the peasant masses, which constituted the vast majority of the population, were convinced that progress toward equality could be made by peaceful, constitutional means.

VII

INDIA AS A SECULAR STATE

Do we believe in a national State which includes people of all religions and shades of opinion and is essentially secular as a State, or do we believe in the religious, theocratic conception of a State which considers people of other faiths as something beyond the pale? That is an odd question to ask, for the idea of a religious or theocratic State was given up by the world some centuries ago and has no place in the mind of the modern man. And yet the question has to be put in India today, for many of us have tried to jump back to a past age.

Speech at Aligarh, 1948.

CHAPTER VII

INDIA AS A SECULAR STATE

THE religious heritage of modern India may be traced back through several thousands of years. The religious inclination and temperament of her people have often been noted. The emergence of India in the mid-twentieth century as a secular state, in any sense, must therefore be regarded as a very significant development. Jawaharlal Nehru's leadership in bringing about this development has been recognized by virtually all observers of the Indian scene. Chester Bowles wrote of Nehru:

> One of his greatest achievements is the creation of a secular state in which the forty-five million Muslims who chose not to go to Pakistan may live peacefully and worship as they please.[1]

D. F. Karaka, one of his severest critics, conceded that to Nehru must go the credit for maintaining the secular character of the Indian state despite the pressures of Hindu communalism.[2]

This chapter deals with Nehru's theory of the secular state as it has been hammered out on the anvil of Indian political experience. The first part is devoted to Nehru's understanding of the ideal of the secular state. The second part sets forth Nehru's ideas regarding some of the specific areas in which the ideal of the secular state must be applied in India.

THE IDEAL OF THE SECULAR STATE

Definition of the secular state. Nehru has been careful to emphasize that the concept of the secular state is an *ideal* to be striven for. As such it goes beyond laws and constitutions, although these are fundamental and must be in consonance with the ideal if it is to be attained. But the ideal of the secular state ultimately reaches out to embrace the attitudes of groups and individuals toward those of other religions. Thus, Nehru

[1] Bowles, *Ambassador's Report*, p. 104.
[2] D. F. Karaka, 'God is absent from Nehru's Five Year Plans', *The Current*, Vol. VI, No. 1 (September 22, 1954), p. 10.

deprecated actions on the part of certain Hindus which resulted
in a feeling of apprehension in the minds of Indian Christians.

> Anything that creates such an apprehension in the minds of any
> group in India is to be deprecated. It tends to disturb and it is
> opposed to our secular ideal.[1]

Not to consider any of the religious minorities as much a part
of India as anyone else 'immediately leads us away from both
our secular and democratic ideals . . .'[2] The secular state,
then, must be thought of as a social ideal, the realization of
which depends on far more than constitutional provisions.
Nehru regretted that the word 'secular' had to be used, chiefly
for want of a better word. Obviously, it did not mean a State
in which religion as such was discouraged.[3]

The first element in the definition of the secular state is in
terms of state policy—that is, the State must be religiously neu-
tral. One clause of the Karachi Congress resolution on Fundamental Rights, which was drafted by Nehru in 1931, stated
that 'The State shall observe neutrality in regard to all religions'.[4] In 1951, he defined the secular state as one in which
'the State protects all religions, but does not favour one at the
expense of others and does not itself adopt any religion as the
State religion'.[5] The secular state would not in any sense imply
that religion should cease to be an important factor in the private life of the individual. It does mean, however, that 'cardinal
doctrine of modern democratic practice, that is, the separation
of the State from religion . . .'[6]

In November 1953 Nehru referred to the decision of the
Pakistan Constituent Assembly to declare Pakistan an Islamic
Republic in the draft constitution. He stated that this decision
reflects 'a medieval conception, and it is totally opposed to any
democratic conception'.[7] Likewise he deprecated the activities
of Hindu communal groups in India which were agitating for
the creation of a Hindu *Rashtra* or Hindu State. The Hindu
communalists, in their opposition to the Muslim communalists

[1] Nehru, *Circular to the Pradesh Congress Committees*, August, 1954.
[2] *Loc. cit.*
[3] *Loc. cit.*
[4] Resolution on Fundamental Rights and Economic Policy, clause 1 (ix).
Nehru, *The Unity of India*, p. 406.
[5] *The Hindu*, July 17, 1951, p. 4.
[6] Speech in the House of the People. *The Hindu*, April 11, 1950, p. 7.
[7] *The Hindu*, November 16, 1953, p. 1.

and Pakistan, evidenced precisely the same mentality and approach and 'advocate the poisonous thing the Muslim League stood for in the past'.[1] An Islamic Republic and a Hindu State, alike, are diametrically opposed to the democratic ideal of the secular state.

The State may be thought of as the most basic of social institutions, and the first element of Nehru's definition is that it should be separated from religion. The State, however, is not the only social institution which should be dissociated from religion. The second element of Nehru's conception of the secular state is that the process of secularization should extend to other areas of social life. In *Glimpses of World History* Nehru pointed out how the old religions have a tendency to regulate every aspect of day-to-day life.

> Thus Hinduism and Islam, quite apart from their purely religious teachings, lay down social codes and rules about marriage, inheritance, civil and criminal law, political organization, and indeed almost everything else. In other words, they lay down a complete structure for society and try to perpetuate this by giving it religious sanction and authority. Hinduism has gone farthest in this respect by its rigid system of caste.[2]

In a later section are considered Nehru's ideas concerning a uniform civil code, which will ultimately replace the so-called 'personal law' (Hindu Law, Muslim Law, etc.) now in force in India.[3] The idea that a Hindu should be governed by one set of marriage or inheritance laws, and the Muslim who is his nextdoor neighbour should be governed by an entirely separate set of laws, is clearly not in consonance with the ideal of the secular state.

Nehru wrote that the word 'secular' conveyed much more to him than its mere dictionary meaning, especially in relation to social practices.

> Thus, a caste-ridden society is not properly secular. I have no desire to interfere with any person's belief, but where those beliefs become petrified in caste divisions, undoubtedly they affect the social structure of the State.[4]

Hence the ideal of the secular state implies a social structure in

[1] *The Hindu*, July 26, 1948, p. 8.
[2] Nehru, *Glimpses of World History*, p. 736.
[3] *Infra*, p. 162.
[4] Nehru, *Circular to the Pradesh Congress Committees*, August 1954.

which the individual is not subject to the social inequalities imposed by religious sanction.

The third element in Nehru's definition of the secular state is expressed in terms of the fundamental rights of all citizens irrespective of religion. K. T. Ramaswamy emphasized this aspect when he wrote:

> The whole concept of the secular state is based on the elementary truth that the individual is the centre of social organization and not groups—religious or otherwise—and that equal rights should be secured to the citizens through democratic devices.[1]

Nehru drafted the Congress Election Manifesto in July 1951, in preparation for the general elections. The Manifesto stated in part that 'As India is a secular State, every citizen has the same duties, rights, privileges and obligations as any other. He has full freedom to profess and practice his religion'.[2] No person should have any special rights because he adheres to a particular religion; likewise no person should be deprived of his rights because of his religious affiliation.

In 1947 the partition of India was accompanied by violence and a mass exchange of population across the Punjab border. Condemning the agitation of Hindu communalists that Muslims be forced to leave India, Nehru declared that because of India's fundamental conception of the secular state,

> we cannot think in terms of pushing our people from India simply because they happen to belong to any particular religion. That is opposed to a democratic, secular and non-communal conception of a State.[3]

The ideal of the secular state is opposed to the 'religious, theocratic conception of a State which considers people of other faiths as something beyond the pale'.[4]

It was on these grounds also that Nehru criticized the decision that Pakistan should be an Islamic Republic. Such a Constitution inevitably creates two classes of citizens, or two grades of citizenship, with unequal rights and opportunities. Even though the same Constitution provides for the protection of religious minorities, 'the whole conception is that of a superior

[1] K. T. Ramaswamy, 'Secular State in India', *The Hindu*, August 14, 1949, p. 15.
[2] *The Hindu*, July 14, 1951, p. 6.
[3] *The Hindu*, October 13, 1947, p. 6.
[4] Speech at Aligarh, January 24, 1948. Nehru, *Independence and After*, p. 122.

giving some kind of protection to an inferior'.[1] This kind of protection would not even be appreciated by those it is intended to benefit. Psychologically, such a policy could not but create an atmosphere of insecurity and inferiority among the minorities. By contrast, the secular state makes religion irrelevant in defining the obligations, rights, and privileges of citizenship.

In the above paragraphs, three elements or aspects of Nehru's conception of the secular state have been discussed. The three aspects of the definition are interrelated, yet emphasize different facets of the conception. The secular state may be defined in terms of (1) a state policy of neutrality toward all religions; (2) a social structure free from the inequalities imposed by religion; and (3) a state in which all citizens enjoy equal rights, irrespective of religion. Bringing together Nehru's numerous statements on the secular state, a composite definition may be arrived at, as follows: the secular state is a state which is not associated with any particular religion but protects all religions, and in which all individuals enjoy equal political and social rights, status, and opportunities, irrespective of religion or caste background.

Secular state essential in modern times. Nehru has repeatedly emphasized the view that the secular state is the *sine qua non* of modern democratic practice. The idea of a religious or theocratic State 'was given up by the world some centuries ago and has no place in the mind of the modern man'.[2] The religious conception of a state is a throw-back to the medieval period of European history, when Christian nations launched the Crusades in the name of religion. The idea of a religious state recalls the sixteenth century, when it was assumed that the king and his subjects must be adherents of the same faith. As far as modern India is concerned, Nehru declared: 'It is not possible for us to go back to a conception that the world has outlived and that is completely out of tune with modern conceptions'.[3] The secular state should not be thought of as some great and unique achievement.

As a matter of fact, nearly every State in the world is a secular State in practice, even though it may have some old forms attached to it

[1] *The Hindu*, November 16, 1953, p. 1.
[2] Speech at Aligarh, January 24, 1948. Nehru, *Independence and After*, p. 123.
[3] *Loc. cit.*

because no modern civilized State can be other than a secular State.[1]

Nehru ridiculed the tendency of some members of the Constituent Assembly to refer frequently to India's being a secular state as if they had 'done something amazingly generous'.[2] India's decision to adopt the ideal of the secular state should be regarded merely as something which every country does, except a few backward States which are cut off from the main-stream of modern thought.

The necessity of the secular state arises not only out of the demands of modern democratic principles, but also from certain practical considerations.

The Government of a country like India, with many religions that have secured great and devoted followings for generations, can never function satisfactorily in the modern age except on a secular basis.[3]

The democratic approach of the secular state to the problem of religious diversity is also the practical approach, from the point of view of maintaining social stability and harmony among the various religious groups. The progress of a state depends on a certain degree of national unity and solidarity. The granting by the state of a special status to one particular religion would undoubtedly create a feeling of suspicion and apprehension among the adherents of the other faiths. This approach 'is not only wrong in itself but will inevitably lead to friction and trouble'.[4]

Influence of Mahatma Gandhi. Because of Gandhi's lifelong concern over the problems of Hindu-Muslim relations, the question must be raised as to the extent of his influence upon Nehru in the development of the latter's ideas on the secular state. The close association of the two leaders over many years would seem to make some influence almost inevitable.

It is important to recognize that Nehru and Gandhi approached the problem of the relationship between the state and religion from two radically different angles. Gandhi's approach was that of 'a man of religion, a Hindu to the innermost depths

[1] *The Hindu,* July 17, 1951, p. 4.
[2] Speech in the Constituent Assembly, August 12, 1949. India, *Constituent Assembly Debates,* Vol. IX, No. 11, p. 401.
[3] *The Hindu,* September 13, 1950, p. 9.
[4] New Delhi, October 13, 1945. *Important Speeches of Jawaharlal Nehru,* p. 252.

of his being'.[1] While a Hindu, he was nevertheless convinced that all religions were essentially one, and differed only as the various branches of the same tree. In 1928 Gandhi stated that

> after long study and experience I have come to these conclusions, that (1) all religions are true, (2) all religions have some error in them, (3) all religions are almost as dear to me as my own Hinduism. My veneration for other faiths is the same as for my own faith.[2]

Because all religions are one, Gandhi felt that any form of political association based exclusively on adherence to a particular religion was worse than undemocratic. It was a negation of truth.

Gandhi steadfastly opposed all attempts of Muslim League leaders to misrepresent the Indian National Congress as a 'Hindu organization'.[3] The goal of the independence movement was not a Hindu *raj*, but a freedom in which all communities would participate equally. Gandhi conceived of the Congress with its non-communal membership based solely on adult franchise, as 'the *Swaraj* (self-rule) Government in embryo'.[4] By this is meant that the future government of free India should be based on the same secular and non-communal principles on which the Congress was already organized.

Gandhi, in 1940, recognized the fact that if eighty million Muslims desired the partition of India, nothing could prevent it.

> That is the political aspect of it. But what about the religious and the moral which are greater than the political? For, at the bottom of the cry for partition is the belief that Islam is an exclusive brotherhood, and anti-Hindu.[5]

Thus Gandhi opposed the partition proposal on religious grounds, and called it 'an untruth'.

> Partition means a patent untruth. My whole soul rebels against the idea that Hinduism and Islam represent two antagonistic cultures and doctrines. To assent to such a doctrine is for me denial of God. For I believe with my whole soul that the God of the Koran

[1] Nehru, *The Discovery of India*, p. 365.
[2] Quoted in *loc. cit.*
[3] M. K. Gandhi, *To the Hindus and Muslims*, Vol. III of the Gandhi Series, ed. Anand T. Hingorani, Law Journal Press, Allahabad, 1942, p. 412.
[4] *Ibid.*, p. 308.
[5] *Ibid.*, p. 428.

is also the God of the Gita, and that we are all, no matter by what name designated, children of the same God.[1]

The proposal for the creation of a religious or theocratic state was the logical culmination of religious exclusivism, and thus ran directly counter to Gandhi's deepest convictions.

Starting with these religious presuppositions, Gandhi was logically led to the conclusion that the State must be so constructed that all religions can exist peacefully side by side. Therefore the functions of the state must be non-religious, and the government must deal with people as individuals and not as members of religious communities.

> What conflict of interest can there be between Hindus and Muslims in the matter of revenue, sanitation, police, justice, or the use of public conveniences? The difference can only be in religious usage and observances with which a secular State has no concern.[2]

The capacity of the State for serving the people 'stops short of the service of the different faiths, and the services it can render apply to all irrespective of their faiths'.[3] Gandhi wrote that if the free India of the future were ever to live at peace with herself, the State would have to be organized on considerations other than religious.

Gandhi stood in marked contrast to those religious leaders who were presumably led by their religion to demand a communal, religious state. He was basically a man of religion who was led by his religious convictions to declare the necessity of a secular state. But Gandhi must also be contrasted with Nehru, who arrived at similar conclusions regarding the secular state, but by a totally different line of reasoning. Gandhi's starting-point was that of a religious man who, believing all religions to be true, accepted a theory of the state which fits in with this belief; hence the secular state. Nehru's starting-point was that of a practical political thinker and leader steeped in the traditions of Western democracy who, while personally believing all religions to be mostly untrue, had to provide for their freedom to function peacefully without prejudicing the democratic system; hence the secular state. It cannot be said that Gandhi exerted any measurable influence on Nehru in the development

---

[1] *Ibid.*, pp. 415–16.
[2] *Ibid.*, p. 442.
[3] *Ibid.*, p. 443.

of his ideas on the secular state, since their basic approaches were so different. It is probable, however, that Gandhi's conclusions, independently arrived at, did serve to reinforce Nehru's own convictions regarding the necessity of the secular state.

INDIA AS A SECULAR STATE—ACHIEVEMENTS AND PROBLEMS

The first part of this chapter was devoted to a consideration of Nehru's ideal of the secular state. The present part brings into focus Nehru's analysis of the specific areas in which the ideal must be applied in India. In certain of these areas India has already made notable achievements; in others difficult problems still remain.

Certain achievements and problems are quite obvious. For example, the continued presence in India of over forty-five million Muslims is in itself an indication that the ideal has been partially achieved. As Nehru pointed out, there are as many Muslims in India as in any Muslim country excepting Pakistan and Indonesia. The former country is split into two, and thus neither West Pakistan nor East Pakistan has as many Muslims as India.[1] Muslims, Christians, and other non-Hindus continue to occupy important positions in the government, including top-ranking cabinet posts. While recognizing India's achievements in this respect, in other areas it is equally obvious that the ideal is far from realization. The continued existence of communal political parties, despite Nehru's strong opposition, may be cited as an example. In the following pages, a number of aspects of Indian government and society are examined in the light of the ideal of the secular state.

Constitutional foundations of the secular state. Discussing the non-communal nature of the Indian State, Nehru wrote that 'Our Constitution is based on this secular conception and gives freedom to all religions'.[2] While the term 'secular' nowhere appears in the Constitution of India, a reading of the relevant articles will clearly indicate the strong constitutional foundations for the secular state. The most important articles relating to the conception of the secular state may be examined under

[1] Speech in the House of the People, February 18, 1953. *Jawaharlal Nehru's Speeches, 1949–53*, p. 255.
[2] Nehru, *Circular to the Pradesh Congress Committees*, August, 1954.

four headings: (1) the right of the individual to equal treatment by the State irrespective of his religion, (2) the right of the individual to freedom of religion, (3) the rights of religious groups, and (4) the principle that State funds may not be used to promote religion. All of the articles dealt with under these headings are found in Part III, Fundamental Rights, of the Constitution.

The right of the individual to equal treatment by the State irrespective of religion is found in Article 15(1): 'The State shall not discriminate against any citizen on grounds only of religion, race, caste, sex, place of birth or any of them.' This specific guarantee follows the general provisions contained in Article 14 for equality before the law and the equal protection of the laws. Article 16 (1) provides for equality of opportunity 'in matters relating to employment or appointment to any office under the State'. And again, religion and caste are specifically mentioned among the grounds on which there may be no discrimination [Article 16 (2)]. Similarly, no citizen shall be denied admission to any educational institution wholly or partly maintained by State funds on these grounds [Article 29 (2)].

The right of the individual to freedom of religion is guaranteed in Article 25 (1):

> Subject to public order, morality and health... all persons are equally entitled to freedom of conscience and the right freely to profess, practise and propagate religion.

Positively, the individual is given freedom to promote the religion of his choice. Negatively, he may not be compelled to pay taxes 'for the promotion or maintenance of any particular religious denomination' (Article 27).

The rights of religious groups are defined in Article 26 in rather broad language.

> Subject to public order, morality and health, every religious denomination or any section thereof shall have the right—(a) to establish and maintain institutions for religious and charitable purposes; (b) to manage its own affairs in matters of religion; (c) to own and acquire moveable and immovable property; and (d) to administer such property in accordance with law.

The right of religious or linguistic minorities to establish and administer educational institutions is further specified. The State, in its educational grants, shall not discriminate against such institutions on the ground that they are under the management of a minority (Article 30).

The principle that State funds may not be used to promote religion is the basis of Article 28. No religious instruction shall be offered in any educational institution wholly maintained by the State. Furthermore, in any educational institution 'recognized by the State or receiving aid out of State funds', there may be no compulsory attendance at religious instruction or worship. Participation in such religious activities must take place only by the consent of the student or his guardian [Article 18 (3)].

The secular principles of the Indian Constitution may best be judged by contrast with the Constitution of Pakistan. The latter document declares that the State is to be known as 'the Islamic Republic of Pakistan'. Article 32(2) provides that 'a person shall not be qualified for election as President unless he is a Muslim'. The important decision between the principles of joint or communal electorates was left for Parliament to make. The Constitution charges the President with the responsibility for setting up an organization for Islamic research and instruction. Article 198 declares that no law shall be enacted which is repugnant to 'the Injunctions of Islam as laid down in the Holy Quran and Sunnah'.[1]

As Nehru pointed out, the realization of the ideal of the secular state depended on factors going far beyond the letter of the law. Nevertheless, a favourable constitutional framework was an essential prerequisite, and that contained in the Constitution of India was such as to enable Nehru to write: 'India is a secular State'.[2]

Abolition of communal electorates. The Constitution of India abolished the system of separate communal electorates which had prevailed since 1909, and provides for the holding of elections based solely on adult suffrage.

There shall be one general electoral roll for every territorial constituency . . . and no person shall be ineligible for inclusion in any such roll or claim to be included in any special electoral roll

[1] The Constitution of the Islamic Republic of Pakistan, 1956.
[2] Nehru, *Report to the All-India Congress Committee*, 1951, p. 9.

for any such constituency on grounds only of religion, race, caste, sex or any of them (Article 325).

Because of its great importance and because of Nehru's special interest in this feature of the Constitution, it is here given separate treatment.

Under the system introduced in 1909, Muslim candidates could only be elected by separate Muslim electorates to seats reserved for Muslims in the legislatures. Later the system was extended to other communities. An examination of Nehru's statements on the subject reveals four main reasons for his rejection of the principle of separate electorates. First, Nehru held that communal electorates tended to isolate the minority communities from the rest of the country, and thus impeded the development of national unity. A political barrier was set up around them. The process of amalgamation of diverse groups which had been going on in India for centuries was thus reversed. The system solidified religious cleavages at a time when a growing nationalism might well have overcome them. Separate electorates affected the entire structure of social life, and gradually separate trade unions, students' organizations and merchants' chambers were organized on a communal basis.[1] The system made matters worse for the protected minority, for

> the majority electorate lost interest in it and there was little occasion for mutual consideration and adjustment which inevitably take place in a joint electorate when a candidate has to appeal to every group.[2]

A minority group could never effectively exercise the influence which it should exercise if it functioned from behind the barrier imposed by separate electorates. The system gave 'protection' at the cost of forfeiting that fellow-feeling with the majority, which could in time develop. In the final analysis, nothing could really protect a minority more than the goodwill of the majority, for ultimately the will of the majority will prevail in a democracy.[3]

Secondly, Nehru pointed out that separate electorates tended to weaken the minorities by enabling them to lean on artificial

[1] Nehru, The Discovery of India, p. 357.
[2] Ibid., p. 387.
[3] Speech of May 26, 1949. India, Constituent Assembly Debates, 1949, Vol. VIII, p. 330.

props instead of developing self-reliance. An educationally backward group such as the Muslim community was given a false
sense of strength by this system. More attention was paid to
preserving the artificial political props than to real educational,
cultural and economic advance, which alone could make them
permanently strong.[1]

Thirdly, Nehru claimed that separate electorates diverted
attention from the real economic problems of the country.
The system was both a result of communalism, and a stimulus
to its further growth. Thus the evils connected with communalism as a political phenomenon were closely associated with
communal electorates. Separate electorates helped to enable
the communalists to direct public attention to irrelevant religious issues instead of coming to grips with the poverty of the
masses.

Fourthly, communal electorates were opposed to the basic
principles of democracy—Nehru referred to the system as 'the
negation of democracy'.[2] In support of this charge he quoted
the Montagu-Chelmsford Report on India Constitutional Reform (1918), which emphasized the dangers inherent in communal electorates:

> Division by creeds and classes means the creation of political camps
> organized against each other, and teaches men to think as partisans
> and not as citizens . . . We regard any system of communal elec-
> torates, therefore, as a very serious hindrance to the development of
> the self-governing principle.[3]

The four points suggested in the above analysis led Nehru to
conclude with respect to separate electorates that 'undoubtedly
the injury they have caused to every department of Indian life
has been prodigious'.[4]

In August 1947 the Constituent Assembly considered the problem of political safeguards for minorities. The recommendations were made that all elections would be held on the basis of
joint electorates with reservation of seats in the central and state
legislatures for certain specified minorities. The reservation of
seats would be for a period of ten years, after which the question

---

[1] Speech in the Constituent Assembly (Legislative), April 3, 1948. Nehru,
Independence and After, p. 51.
[2] Nehru, *The Discovery of India*, pp. 357–8.
[3] *Ibid.*, p. 358.
[4] *Loc. cit.*

would be reconsidered. These recommendations of the Advisory Committee on Minorities and Fundamental Rights, of which Nehru was a member, were accepted by the Constituent Assembly and embodied in the draft Constitution. Despite some opposition to the idea, the reservation of seats for minorities had been recommended by the Advisory Committee

> in order that minorities may not feel apprehensive about the effect of a system of unrestricted joint electorates on the quantum of their representation in the legislature.[1]

Nehru referred to the proposed reservation of seats as one of the 'definite communal elements' of the draft Constitution, and expressed the personal view that 'the less reservation there is the better'.[2]

Gradually a number of spokesmen for the various minorities came forward with the proposal that the question of reservation of seats be re-examined. On May 11, 1949, the Advisory Committee passed the resolution of Dr. H. C. Mookherjee: 'That the system of reservation for minorities other than Scheduled Castes in Legislatures be abolished'.[3] Defending this new resolution before the Constituent Assembly, Nehru declared that it was psychologically a good move for the nation and for the world, for 'it shows that we are really sincere about this business of having a secular democracy'.[4] In September 1951 Nehru wrote to the state election committees, urging upon them the importance of the Congress selecting candidates from among the minority communities in adequate numbers. It was a matter both of great practical importance and of honour for the Congress. The decision to abolish separate electorates and reservation of seats meant increased responsibility for the majority community.[5]

Progress toward a uniform civil code. As Nehru pointed out, religions like Hinduism and Islam tend to regulate almost every phase of individual and social activity.[6] Both of these religions

---

[1] India, *Constituent Assembly Debates*, 1949, Vol. VIII, pp. 310–11.
[2] Speech in the Constituent Assembly (Legislative) April 3, 1948. Nehru, *Independence and After*, p. 49.
[3] India, *Constituent Assembly Debates*, 1949, Vol. VIII, pp. 310–11. Under the Constitution as ratified, there is reservation of seats for Scheduled Castes and Tribes and Anglo-Indians for a period of ten years.
[4] *Ibid.*, p. 332.
[5] *The Hindu*, September 27, 1951, p. 5.
[6] *Supra*, p. 151.

developed complicated systems of personal law governing marriage, divorce, inheritance, etc. With the coming of British rule to India, Hindu law and Muslim law were taken over into the judicial system which was organized on the British pattern. The courts delivered their judgments on the basis of the communal law applicable to each individual. Thus, on a question of inheritance rights, a Hindu, a Muslim and a Christian would each have a separate and very different law. This situation, which has continued to the present, clearly militates against the ideal of the secular state. Thus Article 44 of the Constitution, included among the Directive Principles of State Policy, asserts that 'The State shall endeavour to secure for the citizens a uniform civil code throughout the territory of India'.

However, even Hindu law is not uniform throughout India. Baroda has a Hindu Code different from that of the rest of India. The Hindu law prevailing in Kerala and Mysore differs in the matter of women's property rights from that of the other states. There are two principal schools of Hindu law: (1) the Dayabhaga school, which prevails in Bengal and Assam, and (2) the Mitakshara school, with four main subdivisions, which prevails throughout the rest of India. The two schools differ notably in the matter of joint family property, and succession and inheritance laws.[1]

The Hindu Code Bill which was drafted by the Government of India sought to codify and modify the Hindu law in regard to eight main subjects: Marriage, adoption, guardianship, joint family property, women's property, intestate succession, testamentary succession, and maintenance. It was an effort to introduce uniformity into Hindu law, at least. The Hindu Code Bill was introduced in Parliament and encountered considerable opposition. The most communally-minded Hindus regarded their personal law as sacred, a part of their religion, and thus not something to be tampered with by legislation. In his statements Nehru emphasized the socially progressive aspects of the Bill.

Thus, the Hindu Code Bill, which has given rise to so much argument, became a symbol of the conflict between progress and reaction in the social domain. I do not refer to any particular clause of

[1] S. V. Gupte, *Hindu Law in British India*, N. M. Yripath Ltd., Bombay, 1947, p. 27.

11

that Bill, . . . but rather to the spirit underlying that Bill. This was a spirit of liberation and of freeing our people and, more especially, our womenfolk, from outworn customs and shackles that bound them.[1]

On September 26, 1951, Nehru announced in Parliament that further consideration of the Hindu Code Bill would be adjourned. While shortness of time was pleaded as the chief reason for this decision, many observers felt that the Government was responding to the pressure of public opinion against the Bill.[2] In the general elections campaign of 1951–52, however, Nehru took a strong stand on the issue, and repeatedly declared that he would never disown the Hindu Code Bill. The decision was made to reintroduce the main parts of the Code as separate bills; first, the Hindu Marriage and Divorce Bill was introduced and later the Hindu Minority and Guardianship Bill.

Nehru pointed out that in the past, Hindu society demonstrated a great capacity for change and adaptation to new circumstances, and it was this quality which gave a certain stability to society.[3] Social usages changed in accordance with the needs of the times, but with the coming of the British, Hindu law assumed a certain rigidity. The British, in establishing the judicial system, consulted the *pandits* about Hindu law and the *maulvis* about Muslim law. These learned men, steeped in past traditions, naturally gave what had been written down centuries ago, although many things had already been changed by custom. As Nehru stated on an earlier occasion,

if the British had not stopped the evolution of Hindu customs, by now they would have changed for the better and there would have been no need for bringing forward the Hindu Code Bill.[4]

The rigidity of Hindu law today could not be eliminated by custom; now it was necessary to resort to legislation.

Nehru declared that the extreme reverence with which some people regarded their personal law, whether Hindu or Muslim or any other personal law, seemed to him to be 'completely misplaced'.[5] The attempt to extend the sphere of religion to all of

[1] Speech of October 18, 1951, *Presidential Address to the Indian National Congress*, pp. 9-10.
[2] *The Hindu*, September 27, 1951, p. 4.
[3] Speech in the House of the People. *The Times of India*, September 16, 1954, p.11.
[4] *The Hindu*, December 10, 1951, p. 1.
[5] *The Times of India*, September 16, 1954, p. 11.

the minute and changing situations in society would probably result in the weakening of the basic concepts of that religion. Giving religious sanction to rigid social usages which increasingly came into conflict with changing modern conditions would ultimately discredit that particular religion. Nehru referred to a Muslim scholar who had advanced the interpretation that Muslim personal law was in no sense an essential part of Islam.

Nehru considered it essential that India should progress toward a certain uniformity in social usages, in the interest of national unity. The process had been begun in the Hindu community itself, and must be extended to bring together the various communities of the country.[1] Nehru stated that a uniform civil code which would apply to everybody was without a doubt the eventual goal. Nevertheless, 'I do not think that at the present moment the time is ripe in India for me to try to push it through'.[2] Arguments that a uniform civil code should be introduced immediately might appear very progressive, but only resulted in hindering the small steps in that direction which could be taken now.

In December 1954 vigorous debate was waged in Parliament over the Hindu Marriage and Divorce Bill, the first instalment of the old Hindu Code Bill. Mr. S. Mahanty, a member of the communal Ganatantra Parishad, declared that to single out Hindu society for reform, from among the several communities of India, was 'discriminatory and against the principle underlying a secular State and the Indian Constitution'.[3] *The Hindu* editorially criticized Nehru's Government for changing the basic purpose of the legislation. The Hindu Code Committee was originally set up to codify and simplify Hindu law, but over a period of years the accent was gradually shifted to social reformism in accordance with 'progressive' ideas. The Government has not framed a uniform civil code for 'political reasons', meaning deference to the feelings of the Muslims and other communities. But the Government should recognize the fact that the Hindus are no more mentally or emotionally prepared for such reformist legislation than are the other communities.[4]

[1] *Loc. cit.*
[2] *Loc. cit.*
[3] *The Hindu*, December 9, 1954, p. 7.
[4] *The Hindu*, December 10, 1954, p. 4.

Despite such criticism, the Hindu Marriage Bill and other parts of the old Hindu Code Bill have been passed by the Indian Parliament.[1] Although India was advancing toward a uniform civil code, the progress was slow, and the biggest hurdle (the modification of Muslim personal law) was yet to be met.

Caste and the secular state. In the discussion of the ideal of the secular state, it was pointed out that one element of Nehru's definition dealt with the effect of religion on the social setup.[2] Nehru held that a truly secular state would imply a social structure in which the individual would not be subject to the social inequalities imposed by religious sanctions. 'Thus, a caste-ridden society is not properly secular.'[3] The caste system constitutes a formidable obstacle to the realization of the ideal in India.

Caste has been responsible for greatly weakening India's civilization throughout her long history, according to Nehru's analysis. The caste system in the early centuries had a certain flexibility, but later, 'along with the growth of rigidity in the caste system grew rigidity of mind, and the creative energy of the race faded away'.[4] Nehru attributed the progressive decline of Indian civilization around 1000 A.D. to a shrinking economy, which was in turn 'the inevitable result of the growing rigidity and exclusiveness of the Indian social structure'.[5]

Nehru pointed out that the caste system has demonstrated a remarkable tenacity in the face of many attempts to eradicate or reform it.[6] Numerous reformers and movements have arisen to challenge caste, but none have thus far succeeded. The usual pattern is that 'rebels against caste have drawn many followers, and yet in course of time their group has itself become a caste'.[7] It is only today that caste is seriously threatened. Having withstood the impact of Buddhism, Islam, and innumerable Hindu reformers, the caste system is now confronted by 'basic economic changes which have shaken up the whole fabric of Indian

[1] *The Hindu*, December 17, 1954, p. 7. The reference to divorce in the title of the Bill was deleted on the same day the Bill was passed.
[2] *Supra*, pp. 151-2.
[3] Nehru, *Circular to the Pradesh Congress Committees*, August, 1954.
[4] Nehru, *The Discovery of India*, p. 86.
[5] *Ibid.*, p. 221.
[6] *Ibid.*, pp. 221-2.
[7] *Ibid.*, p. 112.

society and are likely to upset it completely'.[1] Industrialization will inevitably affect the group pattern on which Indian society has been organized.

The Constitution of India marked a great step forward with the abolition of untouchability. In Article 17 it is stated:

> 'Untouchability' is abolished and its practice in any form is forbidden. The enforcement of any disability arising out of 'untouchability' shall be an offence punishable in accordance with law.

It is elsewhere stated that no citizen, on grounds of religion, race, caste, sex or place of birth, should be denied access to shops, restaurants, etc., or the use of public wells, bathing ghats, or roads, etc.[2]

Among the Directive Principles of State Policy is the undertaking to promote the educational and economic interests of the Scheduled Castes, Scheduled Tribes, and other weaker sections of the population.[3] This article is in keeping with Nehru's repeated statements that the most effective way to aid the backward classes was not by constitutional devices such as reserved seats, but by strengthening them educationally and economically so that they could stand on their own feet.[4] As Nehru expressed it in 1944:

> Therefore not only must equal opportunities be given to all, but special opportunities for educational, economic, and cultural growth must be given to backward groups so as to enable them to catch up to those who are ahead of them.[5]

Undoubtedly, in recent years much good work has been done in this regard by the Harijan Welfare Departments of the various state governments.[6] The measures undertaken by these departments are numerous and varied: provision of house-sites, wells, sanitary amenities, burial grounds, and the leasing of land for cultivation for the eligible communities. In the field of education, Harijan Welfare Departments maintain special schools and hostels, and provide scholarships, stipends and boarding grants.[7]

---

[1] *Ibid.*, p. 242.
[2] Article 15 (2).
[3] *Ibid.*, Article 46.
[4] *Supra*, pp. 160-1.
[5] Nehru, *The Discovery of India*, p. 533.
[6] *Harijan* literally means 'people of God' and was the term which Gandhi applied to the outcaste groups.
[7] *Administration Report of the Harijan Welfare Department, 1951–52*, Government Press, Madras.

An interesting situation developed in Madras State over the question of special concessions and privileges for the backward classes. The Government of Madras State issued a Government Order making reservations in educational institutions for certain classes and communities. The High Court of Madras declared that this Order was contrary to both the letter and the spirit of the Constitution. In particular it violated Article 29 (2), which states:

> No citizen shall be denied admission into any educational institution maintained by the State or receiving aid out of State funds on grounds only of religion, race, caste, language or any of them.

In order to remove the problem created by the ruling of the Madras High Court, the decision was made by the Central Government to propose an amendment to the Constitution. The insertion of Article 15 (4) was one of the several changes brought about by the Constitution (First Amendment) Act of 1951. The amendment is as follows:

> Nothing in this article or in clause (2) of article 29 shall prevent the State from making any special provision for the advancement of any socially and educationally backward classes of citizens or for the Scheduled Castes and Scheduled Tribes.

The amendment, as Nehru remarked, was essentially the giving up of a strict interpretation of equality, [Article 15 (1)] in favour of the gradual elimination of the inequalities to which the backward classes had been subjected.

In Nehru's speeches in Parliament in defence of this amendment, he conceded the logical soundness of the Madras High Court's argument.

> That is to say, if communities as such are brought into the picture, it does go against certain explicit or implied provisions of the Constitution.[1]

Nevertheless, the fact was that certain communities were socially, educationally, and economically backward, and something had to be done for them. In attempting to give them special opportunities, the Government came up against constitutional provisions regarding equality and non-discrimination. In raising the backward classes equality was the ultimate goal, but the

[1] Speech in the House of the People, May 29, 1951. *Jawaharlal Nehru's Speeches, 1949–53*, p. 517.

paradox was that 'in trying to attain equality we came up against certain principles of equality laid down in the Constitution'.[1]

While aiming ultimately at a casteless society in which individuals do not think in terms of group loyalties but of the country at large, the Government still could not ignore the present divisions and fissures in Indian social life. Nehru stated that some members of the Select Committee, while approving of the object of the amendment, feared that the provision 'would be abused and utilized for the benefit of the very communal divisions that have done us so much injury'.[2] However, Nehru denied that this amendment constituted a 'communal approach' to the problem of backwardness.

Nehru expressed his dislike of the words 'backward classes of citizens', even though they occurred in his amendment. He introduced an element of confusion into his argument by declaring:

> What I mean is this: it is the backward individual citizen that we should help. Why should we brand groups and classes as backward and forward? It is a fact that certain groups or classes are backward but I do not wish to brand them as such or treat them as such.[3]

The fact remained that the amendment envisaged aid to the socially and educationally backward people as communities and not as individuals.

Many observers have questioned the wisdom of this decision. First, it is claimed that aid on the basis of communities does tend to perpetuate caste differences. Harijan and Depressed Classes' schools, hostels, and colonies maintained by the Government still keep the Harijans segregated from the rest of the population. Secondly, it is claimed that religious discrimination is exercised in granting aid to the backward classes. Thus, the Christian members of the Indian Parliament in a memorandum placed before the Prime Minister and others, stated:

> A great source of distress to the Christian community has been the refusal, by almost all the State Governments, to give to Harijan converts to Christianity the educational, social and economic assistance which is being given to Hindu Harijans.[4]

[1] *Ibid.*, p. 518.
[2] *Ibid.*, p. 519.
[3] Speech in the House of the People, May 18, 1951. *Jawaharlal Nehru's Speeches, 1949–53*, p. 512.
[4] *The National Christian Council Review*, Vol. LXXI, No. 3 (March 1951), p. 105.

Harijan converts to Christianity, by and large, are just as backward educationally and economically as Hindu Harijans. Some improvement in this situation has been noted since 1951.

Thirdly, some have pointed out that in many cases there is no correlation between caste and economic status.

> The continuance of special economic privileges for Harijans has led to anomalies which should have no place in a democratic setup, for many continue to receive benefits by virtue of their birth in a Harijan 'caste' irrespective of their economic status, while others in real distress are deprived of state help because of their traditionally high 'caste'.[1]

Fourthly, some observers assert that the present approach violates one of the cardinal principles of the secular state, namely that the State deals with its citizens primarily as individuals and not as groups.[2] Many feel that the effective abolition of the social evils connected with caste will not come until the State deals with the problem by a radically different approach.

The question of cow slaughter. The Hindu's veneration for the cow has given rise to an interesting problem relating to the secular state. Gandhi once referred to himself as 'a worshipper of the cow whom I regard with the same veneration as I regard my mother'.[3] The slaughter of cows by beef-eating Muslims has long been a source of communal tension and conflict. Gandhi, despite his great love for the cow, nevertheless asserted that Muslims should have full freedom to slaughter cows, as long as it was done in a way that would not offend the susceptibilities of their Hindu neighbours. He felt that this concession was indispensable for communal harmony.

Since independence the question of anti-cow-slaughter legislation has been raised on a number of occasions. Among the Directive Principles of State Policy of the Constitution is an article directing the State to take steps for 'prohibiting the slaughter of cows and calves and other milch and draught cattle'.[4] The Hindu communal parties and a few Congressmen have been extremely active in agitating for such legislation by Parliament in the face of Nehru's strong opposition. Mr. Seth Govind Das (a member of the Congress Party) introduced the

[1] *The Guardian*, Madras, Vol. XXXII, No. 12 (March 25, 1954), p. 90.
[2] *Supra*, p. 152.
[3] *Harijan*, April 27, 1940. *To the Hindus and Muslims*, p. 477.
[4] Article 48.

Indian Cattle Preservation Bill in the Lok Sabha in 1952. The motion for the consideration of the Bill was discussed several times, but was not voted on until April 1955.[1] In the lively debate which preceded the voting, Nehru declared that he was prepared to stake his Prime Ministership on the issue, and that his Government would never accept such a Bill. Ninety-five members voted against and only twelve for the motion. Significantly, among the twelve were Mr. Purshottamdas Tandon, former president of the Congress, and another Congressman, Pandit Thakurdas Bhargava.

Nehru's position on this question could be summarized under three points. First, he held that it was clearly a matter for the State Governments to deal with, not the Centre. The Attorney-General had given his opinion that the subject came essentially within the competence of the State Legislatures. Nehru emphasized that local sentiments and feelings should be taken into consideration on the issue. For example, an all-India act banning cow slaughter would naturally apply to the North-West Frontier hills and tribal areas, where there was already unrest and agitation against the Government of India. A serious situation would be created among the Muslim tribesmen.[2] The United Provinces Government had recently decided to ban cow slaughter throughout the state. While it was for the State to make its own decision on the issue, Nehru personally felt, for other reasons, that it was a wrong step.

The second point is that Nehru emphasized the approach of practical economics, as opposed to the sentimental or religious approach. From the point of view of agricultural economics, 'proper cattle preservation and improvement of breeds and increase in milk supply are of high importance to the country'.[3] But the problem was not usually viewed from this angle. Nehru declared that religion has been misapplied and misplaced with regard to the cow.[4] Some of India's old traditions and customs definitely impeded clear thinking on economic problems. Nehru asserted that sometimes the anti-cow-slaughter agitations were not even religious, but were politically inspired.

Thirdly, Nehru emphasized a constructive approach as

[1] *The Hindu*, April 4, 1955, p. 1.
[2] *The Hindu*, April 11, 1955, p. 6.
[3] Nehru, *Report to the All India Congress Committee*, 1951, p. 13.
[4] *The Hindu*, March 5, 1951, p. 1.

opposed to negative measures. Anti-cow-slaughter legislation is a negative action which would probably result only in an increase in the great number of diseased and weak cattle.[1] In many cases cow slaughter takes place because milkmen in the large cities find it unprofitable to keep cows when they go dry.[2] This was a problem which would have to be met positively. The slaughter of milch cows and their progeny (as distinguished from draught cattle) should be stopped, Nehru asserted, purely because of their economic value. But this could only be done through a constructive programme.[3]

Leaders of the Hindu Mahasabha, Ram Rajya Parishad, and Jan Sangh appealed to the people in April 1955 to organize demonstrations to protest against Nehru's defiance of the 'national will' regarding cow protection. Some observers felt that although Nehru's opposition to bans on cow slaughter was undoubtedly firm and unequivocal, the arguments he publicly advanced to support his position were not the most important ones. It is true that Nehru has vaguely referred, in the context of this issue, to the fact that many of India's social habits 'are separatist and do not encourage the community outlook'.[4] But in his public statements he has generally ignored the threat to the secular state inherent in the legislation now demanded. Accepting Nehru's contention that the agitation is based chiefly on sentimental and religious, not economic, considerations, the question of principle becomes the following: In a secular state should the coercive power of the state be used to impose upon all citizens the taboos of one particular religion? It is interesting to note that, in contrast with Nehru's apparent hedging on the issue, the Communist Party leader stated that 'the Bill sponsored by Seth Govind Das was obscurantist and motivated by sheer communalism'.[5]

The total impact of Nehru's deep convictions regarding the secular state on Indian political life is difficult to measure. Undoubtedly, many in India have accepted the principle out of loyalty to Nehru but are without a very clear understanding of it. This much is certain: India's emergence in the mid-twentieth

[1] *Loc. cit.*
[2] Letter of August 20, 1954. Nehru, *Letters to the P.C.C. Presidents*, p. 25.
[3] Letter to Mr. Purshottamdas Tandon. *The Hindu*, April 11, 1955, p. 6.
[4] Nehru, *Report to the All India Congress Committee*, 1951, p. 13.
[5] *The Hindu*, April 4, 1955, p. 4.

century as a secular state in any sense cannot be understood apart from this impact. Through a period when religious hostility ran high Nehru's commitment to the ideal of the secular state did not and has not wavered.

Nehru's thought on the secular state may here be summed up briefly. The secular state is a state which protects all religions equally but favours none at the expense of the others. It is a state which recognizes equal rights, privileges, and duties as belonging to all citizens irrespective of their religion or caste. The secular state is not only a cardinal principle of modern democratic practice, but is also necessary in order to maintain a sense of national unity within a country. Gandhi arrived at a similar conception of the secular state, but proceeded by a very different line of reasoning. As contrasted with Nehru's secular philosophy of life, Gandhi believed that all religions were equally true, and therefore saw no reason for the state to discriminate and favour one above the rest.

Communalism is the tendency of religious groups to function as such in politics, and Nehru viewed it as the greatest obstacle to the secular state in India. The long history of communalism finally led to the partition of India. A new state, Pakistan, declared itself an Islamic Republic, and communalists in India sought to turn their country into a Hindu State.

In applying his concept of the secular state to Indian conditions, Nehru has had to deal with a number of issues unknown to European and American political experience. He opposed the principle of communal electorates which had prevailed prior to independence. By allowing Muslims to vote only for Muslim candidates, the system had encouraged separatist feelings, and had encouraged the Muslims and other minorities to think of themselves in terms of communities and not as Indians. Separate electorates were abolished by the Constitution framed after independence. Communal civil codes, differing widely on many points, posed another problem for the secular state. Nehru urged the eventual creation of a uniform civil code, whereby Hindus, Muslims, and Christians would come under the same marriage, inheritance, and guardianship laws. As a first step toward this objective, the Hindu Code Bill was drafted in order to unify Hindu personal law.

The institution of caste, with its semi-religious sanctions, further threatened Nehru's ideal of the secular state. Untouchability was abolished by the Constitution, and the State was committed to improving the lot of the Harijans by positive measures to increase their cultural, educational and economic opportunities. But new questions and problems arose when the State conferred these advantages on people not as individuals but as castes.

The Hindu custom of venerating the cow gave rise to another challenge to the secular state. Hindu political parties agitated for laws banning cow slaughter, and Nehru opposed this attempt to use the State in order to enforce the taboos of one particular religion.

VIII

NEHRU AS INTERPRETER

WE are in the middle of the twentieth century and I doubt if these concepts can apply *in vacuo* to any given situation in India. My Government and I fully accept and endorse democratic values but one should avoid thinking merely in terms of phrases and clichés. . . .

Speech in Parliament, 1952.

CHAPTER VIII

NEHRU AS INTERPRETER

IN the foregoing chapters I have endeavoured to present as clearly as possible Nehru's thought regarding some of the basic problems of democracy. His ideas on the meaning of democracy, fundamental rights, economic democracy, and the secular state have been discussed, not as abstract ideas, but in the context of India's peculiar social, economic and political situation. The first part of the present chapter will attempt to draw together the threads of this discussion by a consideration of two generalizations which have emerged from this study. The generalizations relate to the major emphases which characterize Nehru's political thinking.

The second part of this chapter will attempt to evaluate Nehru's democratic thought. Has Nehru made any particular contribution to democratic thought, and if so, what is it? Does his thought have significant implications for other Asian countries as well as for India? These are the questions, and I shall offer my answers, based on the findings of this study.

Characteristic Emphases of Nehru's Thought

Two important emphases recur frequently in the writings and speeches of Nehru; the first relates to the world conditions in which the democratic state must function, and the second to the nature of the democratic process itself.

Democracy in a changing world. One basic fact which Nehru has emphasized perhaps more than any other is the dynamic changing nature of the modern world, to which democratic theory and practice must adjust. This aspect of Nehru's thought is best expressed in the quotation given in a previous chapter.

A constitution which is unchanging and static—it does not matter how good it is, how perfect it is—is a constitution that has outlived its use. It is in its old age already and gradually approaching its death. A constitution to be living must be growing, must be adaptable, must be flexible, must be change-able.[1]

Nehru told the House of the People that the most effective way of killing the Constitution would be to make it sacred and sacrosanct. The democratic ideas of the eighteenth and nineteenth centuries are very good, but they could not be applied unthinkingly to every situation, for the world has changed, and this is a most fundamental fact.

The doctrine of freedom of the press was evolved at a time when state interference was the biggest threat to the independence of the press. Nehru suggested that today the growth of huge newspaper chains controlled by vested interests constituted one of the gravest dangers. The entire situation had changed, and yet some people continued to think of freedom of the press in terms of eighteenth century conditions.

Nehru pointed out that an important aspect of the changing times is the awakening of the masses to the possibilities of material improvement of their lot. The masses are still living in poverty, for the most part, but they are no longer content to continue in these circumstances. This new consciousness of the masses has revolutionary implications for the democratic state, for rival authoritarian systems will surely step in if democracy fails to 'deliver the goods'.

The new consciousness of the masses has become most evident in the demand for land reform in Asia. Dynamic forces are now challenging what had been taken for granted for hundreds of years. If these forces are not recognized and dealt with properly, Nehru warned, the stability of the social structure itself will be endangered. If the democratic state seeks to protect individual rights without regard to the demand for greater economic equality, it jeopardizes its own future.

Nehru has also pointed out a number of areas in which recent technological advances have made adjustments in democratic theory necessary. The development of new media of mass communication has tended to produce the 'de-individualization of the individual'. In a society dominated by the machine, man himself tends to respond like a machine. The highly organized and concentrated media of mass communication tend to

[1] Speech in the House of the People, May 29, 1951. *Jawaharlal Nehru's Speeches, 1949–53*, p. 525.

regiment public opinion. In such a society the non-conformist may be as badly off as if there were no freedom of expression. Hence the old and accepted principles of democracy must be re-examined in the light of changing conditions.

The harnessing of atomic energy and other great technological advances have opened up entirely new areas for industrial development. Nehru criticized socialists and communists whose theories largely presupposed a static technology. The socialists called for immediate nationalization of the existing means of production, not realizing that these were already becoming obsolete. Nehru held that it was far wiser for the State to invest its limited financial resources in these new industries, rather than to pay out huge sums for compensation in order to acquire something which was fast becoming out of date. Democratic socialism would have to adjust itself to the vitally new conditions which were emerging.

The most characteristic emphasis of Nehru's political thought is this: that the changing conditions of modern times require of each new generation that it rethink and redefine its political faith. Static political creeds are not only wrong but dangerous. A living constitution 'must be growing, must be adaptable, must be flexible, must be changeable'.[1]

Conflict and balance. A second characteristic of Nehru's thinking on democracy, as revealed by this study, is his emphasis on conflict and balance. The democratic process, as Nehru conceives of it, is largely a matter of adjusting and balancing certain principles which, while valid in themselves, tend to conflict with one another. The corollary of this conception is that most of the problems of democracy are insoluble by any formula; their solution lies largely in striking the right balance between contradictory emphases.

In a democratic state, freedom and equality are both undoubtedly of great importance. Nevertheless, there is a certain conflict between the two concepts, for 'when you bring equality it may interfere with somebody's freedom'.[2] In the Indian Constitution, both the static principles embodied in the Fundamental Rights and the dynamic concept of the Directive Principles were essential to the development of democracy.

[1] *Loc. cit.*
[2] Nehru, *Visit to America*, p. 136.

12

Nevertheless, 'sometimes it might so happen that the dynamic movement and the static concept do not quite fit in with each other'.[1] The solution of the problem lies in finding a workable *balance* of the two principles.

The concept of individual freedom also comes into conflict with the idea of order in society. Unless the State is perfect and every individual is perfect, the conflict will be present. Nevertheless, in a democratic society, neither concept may be defined without reference to the other; in other words, a balance must be struck. If individual rights are not exercised responsibly and with due consideration for the rights of others, the State must use its coercive power to find that balance between individual freedom and social freedom.

In the modern world, individual freedom increasingly comes into conflict with the trend toward centralization. Centralized authority today is inevitable, whether it is in the big business corporation, the trade union, or the State. Nehru does not view this as a necessary evil to be grimly endured; centralization has become the trend because it produces the results required. Centralized authority is not only inevitable in the larger scheme of modern life, but necessary and desirable for the economic reconstruction of India. Only through a 'democratically planned collectivism' can economic progress be effected. Nevertheless, a conflict is thus created, for 'we want to preserve the freedom of the individual, and at the same time we cannot escape centralization in modern society. How to balance the two?'[2] The answer could only be framed in terms of 'balance'.

Conflict seems to be inherent even in the definition of democracy. The principle of majority rule is certainly as essential an element of democracy as individual rights, yet there is a logical conflict between the two ideas. Majority rule might be exercised in a manner detrimental to the rights of minorities or non-conformist individuals. Similarly, the concept of individual rights, if considered in isolation and pressed to its logical conclusion, might result in a few thwarting the will of the majority.

Leadership in a democracy poses many problems, and one of them is the conflict which often arises between the

---

[1] Speech in the House of the People, May 16, 1951. *Jawaharlal Nehru's Speeches, 1949–53*, p. 492.
[2] Cousins, *Talks with Nehru*, pp. 23–4.

conscientious leader's ideals and the demands of the people in any given situation. The leader dare not disregard completely the will of the majority; neither should he surrender his own convictions regarding truth. Inevitably, some kind of compromise or balance must be arrived at; it may be a good compromise 'if it is always looking at that truth and trying to take you there'.[1]

Thus, one of Nehru's most frequently recurring emphases is that the democratic system of government is largely a question of conflict and balance. Democracy must be viewed as a composite theory containing a number of essential elements, some of which conflict with one another. In the normal course of the democratic process these conflicting elements are balanced peacefully. Sometimes the balance is more in favour of one element; under different circumstances the balance is shifted toward the other side. Thus, most of the problems of democracy have no permanent solutions. As the inherent conflicts assume different forms, new balances must be struck.

NEHRU AS A POLITICAL THINKER

As was pointed out in the Preface of this book, Nehru could in no sense be regarded *primarily* as a political philosopher. He is a political leader, a politician, who has read widely and thought deeply about the problems of democracy. His philosophical bent of mind has enabled him to interpret day-to-day problems with a certain theoretical perspective. His political theory is essentially eclectic, drawn from the diverse intellectual currents of the nineteenth and twentieth centuries. A man of great sensitivity, Nehru has absorbed and combined in himself many of the dominant impulses and ideas of modern democratic thought.

While Nehru has devoted his life far more to the *practice* than to the *theory* of politics, he has made a significant contribution in the latter field as well as in the former. Nehru's distinctive contribution to political philosophy lies in his application of democratic ideas to Indian conditions. The political theories which were largely derived from the West had to be made meaningful in an entirely different cultural and political context. The basic conceptions had to be worked out in relation to problems which were considerably different from those of

[1] India, *Constituent Assembly Debates*, 1949, Vol. II, Part II, pp. 1229-30.

Europe and America. The preceding chapters have shown, essentially, Nehru's attempts to make these political ideas relevant to the needs of the Indian scene.

Nehru found in Indian conditions certain factors which made impossible a blind copying of Western theories regarding fundamental rights. Thus the rights of personal liberty and freedom of the press could not be considered in a vacuum, nor in relation to conditions prevailing a hundred years ago in countries thousands of miles away. They had to be interpreted in terms of present-day conditions in India. It was necessary to take into account the facts of the partition of India, communist and communal violence and disturbances, an uneasy truce with Pakistan, the peculiar characteristics of the modern Indian press, and many others circumstances.

The socialist ideas embodied in Nehru's theory of economic democracy were developed in a Europe which had largely solved the problem of production through an expanding capitalism. Socialism addressed itself principally to the problem of distribution. Nehru sought to apply the basic principles of socialism to an underdeveloped country in which production was still the greatest economic problem. The shouting of doctrinaire slogans about nationalizing everything in sight solved no problems; the principles of democratic socialism would have to be adapted to Indian conditions.

Furthermore, the doctrines of socialism originated in an industrialized society, but had to be interpreted by Nehru in an agricultural country in which the demand for greater equality in land was the dominant factor in the thinking of the masses. Socialism had provided theories to show that value was created by society as a whole, but Nehru had to adapt these theories to the specific problems of legislation abolishing the big landed estates.

The concept of the secular state was first developed in terms of 'separation of church and state'. The concept slowly evolved in the eighteenth and nineteenth centuries out of definite historical situations. Nehru's theory of the secular state becomes a twentieth-century interpretation of the concept in terms of the Indian state and society. The theory of the secular state in India raises many problems unknown to Western political experience, such as separate electorates for the various religious communities, communal personal laws, the caste system, agitation for laws banning cow slaughter, and so forth. Nehru's significant contribution, then, lies in this application and adaptation of democratic ideas to Indian politics.

Jawaharlal Nehru may justly be regarded as the foremost interpreter of liberal democracy that Asia has produced. Other Indian writers, such as Vivekanda, Tagore, and Aurobindo, gave relatively little attention to political subjects, and none of them grappled with the problems of democracy in independent India. Gandhi did not claim to believe in Western democracy, and was thus in no position to interpret it to India.

Elsewhere in Asia, Sun Yat-sen stands out as one who, struggling against enormous odds, attempted to apply democratic conceptions to the politics and government of his country. While the final evaluation of his work must rest with history, at present a totalitarian Communist regime in China defies the principles which Dr. Sun patiently expounded during his lifetime. Free India is committed to parliamentary democracy by an excellent Constitution, but written constitutions do not tell the whole story. The future of democracy in India may depend in large measure on the degree to which Jawaharlal Nehru succeeds in interpreting, applying, and adapting democratic ideas to the political life of this people.

To take the discussion one step further, what of India's position in Asia? Democratic India and totalitarian China confront the peoples of Southeast Asia with alternative systems of government and ways of life. The countries of this area are faced with grave dangers, and the picture is dark indeed in some places. As these lines are being written, President Sukarno has declared that Western-type parliamentary democracy simply does not work in Indonesia. India's continued progress under democracy may well become a decisive factor in this strategic area of the world. Nehru's role as interpreter of democracy to India thus has international overtones as India interprets democracy to Asia.

BIBLIOGRAPHY

A. Books

Anonymous, *Building New India: Selections from M. K. Gandhi, Rabindranath Tagore, Jawaharlal Nehru, S. Radhakrishnan, Vinoba Bhave,* All India Congress Committee, New Delhi, 1954. 97 pp.

——————, *Nehru Abhinandan Granth : A Birthday Book.,* ed. Rajendra Prasad and others, Vishwanath More, Calcutta, 1949. 705 pp.

Banerjee, A. C., *The Constituent Assembly of India,* A. Mukherjee and Co., Calcutta, 1947. xviii, 350 pp.

Banerjee, D. N., *The Future of Democracy and Other Essays,* A. Mukherjee and Co., Calcutta, 1953. 228 pp.

Bowles, Chester, *Ambassador's Report,* Harper and Brothers, New York, 1954. x, 415 pp.

Bright, Jagat S., *Jawaharlal Nehru : A Biographical Study,* The Indian Printing Works, Lahore, 1945. 224 pp.

Brown, D. Mackenzie, *The White Umbrella: Indian Political Thought from Manu to Gandhi,* University of California Press, Berkeley and Los Angeles, 1953. xv, 205 pp.

Campbell-Johnson, Alan, *Mission with Mountbatten,* Robert Hale Ltd., London, 1951. 383 pp.

Coker, Francis W., *Readings in Political Philosophy,* Macmillan Co., New York, 1938. xvi, 717 pp.

Cousins, Norman, *Talks with Nehru: India's Prime Minister Speaks out on the Crisis of Our Time,* Victor Gollancz Ltd., London, 1951. 64 pp. First appeared in *The Saturday Review of Literature,* April 14 and 21, 1951.

Das, Taraknath, *Rabindranath Tagore—His Religious, Social and Political Ideals,* Saraswathy Library, Calcutta, 1932. vii, 55 pp.

Dhawan, Gopinath, *The Political Philosophy of Mahatma Gandhi,* second revised edition, Navajivan Publishing House, Ahmedabad, 1951. viii, 407 pp.

Doabia, H. S., *The Law of Preventive Detention in India: Being an Exhaustive Commentary on the Preventive Detention Act of 1950, as amended up to date, with all the amending Acts, etc.,* Sidh Law House, Simla, 1951. ii, 198 pp.

Dwivedi, R., *The Life and Speeches of Pandit Jawaharlal Nehru,* second edition, Cooperative P. Press, Indore. 59 pp.

Fisher, Margaret W., and Bondurant, Joan V., *Indian Approaches to a Socialist Society,* Indian Press Digests — Monograph Series, No. 2, July 1956. University of California Press, Berkeley. xliii, 105 pp.

Gandhi, Mahatma, *To the Hindus and Muslims,* ed. Anand T. Hingorani, Vol. III of Gandhi Series, Law Journal Press, Allahabad, 1942. 503 pp.

——————, *An Autobiography, or The Story of My Experiments with Truth*. Translated from the original Gujarati by Mahadev Desai, Navajivan Publishing House, Ahmedabad, 1948. viii, 640 pp.

Ghose, Arabindo, *The Spirit and Form of Indian Policy*, Arya Publishing House, Calcutta, 1947. 91 pp.

Gunther, John, *Inside Asia*, Harper and Brothers, New York, 1938. 637 pp.

Gupte, S. V., *Hindu Law in British India*, N. M. Tripathi Ltd., Bombay, 1947. 1170 pp.

Hutheesing, Krishna, *With No Regrets: Krishna Hutheesing's Autobiography*, Oxford University Press, Bombay, 1944.

Karaka, D. F., *Nehru: The Lotus Eater from Kashmir*, Richard Clay and Co. Ltd., London, 1953. 114 pp.

Kripalani, K. R. *Gandhi, Tagore and Nehru*, second edition, Hindu Kitabs Ltd., Bombay, 1949. 141 pp.

Krishnamurti, Y. G., *Jawaharlal Nehru: the Man and His Ideas*, third edition, Popular Book Depot, Bombay, 1945. xxx, 168 pp.

Linebarger, Paul M.A., *The Political Doctrines of Sun Yat-sen: An Exposition of the San Min Chu I.*, The Johns Hopkins Press, Baltimore, 1937. xiv, 278 pp.

Majid, Abdul, *Jawaharlal Nehru and His Ideas*, The Indian Printing Works, Lahore, 1945. 102 pp.

Mandlekar, B. R., *Musings on Democratic Life in India*, Madhya Pradesh Civil Liberties Union, Nagpur, 1955.

Mao Tse-tung, *On New Democracy*, Foreign Languages Press, Peking, 1954. 84 pp.

Moraes, Frank, *Jawaharlal Nehru: A Biography*, Macmillan Co., New York, 1956. x, 511 pp.

Nehru, Jawaharlal, *Important Speeches of Jawaharlal Nehru; being a collection of most significant speeches delivered by Jawaharlal Nehru from 1922 to 1946*, ed. Jagat S. Bright, second revised enlarged edition, The Indian Printing Works, Lahore, 1946. iv, 396 pp.

——————, *Selected Writings of Jawaharlal Nehru, 1916-1950*, ed. Jagat S. Bright, The Indian Printing Works, New Delhi, no date given. viii, 353 pp.

——————, *India on the March: Statements and Selected Quotations from the Writings of Jawaharlal Nehru; Relevant to the Subject Only, Covering Three Decades of His Political Career, from 1916 to 1946*, ed. Jagat S. Bright, Indian Printing Works, Lahore, 1946. 330 pp.

——————, *Nehru Flings a Challenge*, second edition Extracts of Nehru's Writings, ed. 'A Student', Hamara Hindoostan Publications, Bombay, 1947. xxvii, 140 pp.

——————, *Letters from a Father to His Daughter: Being a brief account of the early days of the world, written for children*, Oxford University Press, Bombay, 1929. 75 pp.

——————, *Soviet Russia: Some Randon Sketches and Impressions*, Chetana Ltd., Bombay, 1929. xii, 132 pp.

——————, *Recent Essays and Writings: on the Future of India, Communalism and other Subjects*, Kitabistan, Allahabad, 1934. 248 pp.

——————, *India and the World*, George Allen and Unwin Ltd., London, 1936. 262 pp.

——————, *China Spain, and the War*, Kitabistan, Allahabad, 1940. 269 pp.

——————, *Toward Freedom: The Autobiography of Jawaharlal Nehru*, John Day Co., New York, 1941. xv, 449 pp.

——————, *Glimpses of World History: being further letters written in prison, and containing a rambling account of history for young people*, John Day Co., New York, 1942. xvi, 993 pp.

——————, *The Discovery of India*, John Day Co., New York, 1946. xi, 595 pp.

——————, *India Rediscovered*. An abridged version of *The Discovery of India*, ed. C. D. Narasimhaiah, Oxford University Press, Bombay, 1954. xxii, 241 pp.

——————, *Eighteen Months in India 1936-1937: Being Further Essays and Writings*, Allahabad Law Journal Press, Allahabad, 1938. viii, 319 pp.

——————, *The Unity of India: Collected Writings 1937-1940*, John Day Co., New York, 1948. 432 pp.

——————, *Mahatma Gandhi*, Signet Press, Calcutta, 1949. 171 pp.

——————, *Nehru on Gandhi*, John Day Co., New York, 1948. x, 150 pp.

——————, *Visit to America*, John Day Co., New York, 1950. vii, 182 pp.

——————, *Independence and After: A Collection of Speeches, 1946-1949*, John Day Co., New York, 1950. 403 pp.

——————, *Jawaharlal Nehru's Speeches 1949-1953*, The Publications Division, Ministry of Information and Broadcasting, Government of India, Calcutta, 1954. x, 586 pp.

Ramachandran, V. G., *The Law of Preventive Detention*, Law Journal Office, Madras, 1954. lxi, 206 pp.

Sabine, George H., *A History of Political Theory*, Henry Holt and Co., New York, 1951. xxi, 934 pp.

Scott, Roland W., *Social Ethics in Modern Hinduism*, Y.M.C.A. Publishing House, Calcutta, 1953. 243 pp.

Sen, Sachin, *The Political Thought of Tagore*, General Printers, Calcutta, 1947. ii, 360 pp.

Seth, Hira Lal, *The Red Star of the East: A Biographical Study of Jawaharlal Nehru*, Hero Publications, Lahore, 1943. 131 pp.

Smith, Wilfred Cantwell, *Modern Islam in India*, Victor Gollancz Ltd., London, 1946. 344 pp.

Srivatsa, *Pandit Jawaharlal Nehru: A Study at Close Quarters*, Dikshit Publishing House, Madras, No date given. 49 pp.

Sun Yat-sen, *The Three Principles of the People*. Translated into English by Frank W. Price, ed. L. T. Chen, Institute of Pacific Relations, Shangahi, 1927. 514 pp.

Tandon, P. D., *Nehru, Your Neighbour*, Signet Press, Calcutta, 1946. xiv, 178 pp.

Tagore, Rabindranath, *Nationalism*, Macmillan, New York, 1917. 159 pp.

Vivekananda, *Modern India*, Advaita Ashrama, Almora, 1923. 43 pp.

Yankey, Grace (Sydenstricker), *Nehru of India*, by Cornelia Spencer (pseud.), John Day Co., New York, 1948. v, 194 pp.

B. PAMPHLETS

Anonymous, *Progress of Land Reform*, The Publications Division, Ministry of Information and Broadcasting, Government of India, Delhi, 1955. 28 pp.

Ghosh, Ajoy, *Communist Answer to Pandit Nehru*, New Age Printing Press, Delhi, 1955. 16 pp.

——————, *Nehru's Socialism—A Hoax*, New Age Printing Press, Delhi, 1955. 16 pp.

Nehru, Jawaharlal, *Presidental Address, Indian National Congress, Fifty-seventh Session*, All India Congress Committee, New Delhi, 1951. 21 pp.

——————, *Presidential Address, Indian National Congress, Fifty-eighth Session*, All India Congress Committee, New Delhi, 1953. 22 pp.

——————, *Presidential Address, Indian National Congress, Fifty-ninth Session*, All India Congress Committee, New Delhi, 1954. 19 pp.

——————, *Report to the All India Congress Committee*, All India Congress Committee, New Delhi, 1951. 20 pp.

——————, *Report to the All India Congress Committee*, All India Congress Committee, New Delhi, 1955. 14 pp.

——————, *Letters to the P.C.C. Presidents*, All India Congress Committee, New Delhi, 1955. 31 pp.

——————, *The Question of Language*, Allahabad Law Journal Press, Allahabad, 1937. 24 pp.

C. ARTICLES AND PERIODICALS

All India Congress Committee Economic Review, Vols. I-VII, All India Congress Committee, New Delhi, 1949-55.

Anonymous, 'The Secular State in India', *National Christian Council Review*, Vol. LXXIV, No. 3 (March 1954), pp. 104–11.

Congress-Bulletin, All India Congress Committee, New Delhi, 1945-1955.

Cousins, Norman, 'Talks with Nehru', *Saturday Review of Literature*, Vol. XXXVI, No. 50 (December 12, 1953), pp. 11-12, 62-4.

Das, T., 'An Indian Examines Nehru', *New American Mercury*, Vol. 72 (February 1951), pp. 168-78.

The Guardian (Madras), Vol. XXXII, 1954.

Hutheesing, Krishna, 'Nehru and Madame Pandit', *Ladies' Home Journal*, Philadelphia, Vol. LXXII, No. 1 (January 1955).

Karaka, D.F., 'God is absent from Nehru's Five Year Plans', *The Current*, Vol. VI, No. 1 (September 22, 1954), p. 10.

Nehru, Jawaharlal, 'Inter-Asian Relations', *India Quarterly*, Vol. II, No. 4 (October-December 1946), pp. 323-7.

—————, 'Foreword' to Mahatma: *Life of Mohandas Karamchand Gandhi*, by D. G. Tendulkar, Vol. I, Vithalbhai K. Jhaveri and D. G. Tendulkar, Bombay, 1951, p. xi-xv.

Norman, Dorothy, 'Jawaharlal Nehru's Book of Job', review of *Independence and After* in *Saturday Review of Literature*, Vol. XXXIII, No. 29 (July 22, 1950), pp. 10-11.

Rama, Rao D. V., 'Land Reform or New Untouchability?', *Swantantra* (Madras), Vol. IX, No. 31 (September 4, 1954), p. 23.

Ramaswamy, K. T., 'Secular State in India', *The Hindu*, August 14, 1949.

Rosenthal, A. M., 'Clues to Jawaharlal Nehru—and to India', *New York Times Magazine* (July 1, 1956), pp. 5, 29-34.

—————, 'Nehru—Still the Searcher', *New York Times Magazine* (December 16, 1956), pp. 14, 45-6.

Roy, M. N., 'Jawaharlal Nehru', *Twentieth Century*, Vol. 151 (February 1952), pp. 137-45.

Smith, Donald E., 'Gandhi and Nehru on the Concept of the Secular State', *Nagpur University Political Science Association Bulletin*, 1954-1955, pp. 20-3.

Swatantra (Madras), 'Socialism from the Wrong End', editorial, Vol. IX, No. 26 (July 31, 1954), p. 4.

—————, (Madras), 'Our Welfare State', editorial, Vol. IX, No. 28 (August 14, 1954), p. 4.

Trumbull, Robert, 'Nehru Answers some Basic Questions', *New York Times Magazine*, (November 11, 1951), pp. 52-7.

D. GOVERNMENT PUBLICATIONS

Administration Report of the Harijan Welfare Department, 1951-52. Government Press, Madras, 1953. 114 pp.

Constituent Assembly of India (Legislative) Debates: Official Report, Government of India Press, New Delhi, 1947-49. 15 vols.

Constituent Assembly Debates: Official Report, Government of India Press, New Delhi, 1946-49. 12 vols.

Constitution of India. Government of India Press, New Delhi, 1951. xviii, 254 pp.

Jawaharlal Nehru: Press Conferences 1953, Government of India Press, New Delhi, 1954. 99 pp.

Legislative Assembly Debates: Official Report, Government of India Press, New Delhi, 1946-47. 13 vols.

Parliamentary Debates: Council of States: Official Report, Government of India Press, New Delhi, 1952-55.

Parliamentary Debates : House of People: Official Report, Government of India Press, New Delhi, 1952-55.

Parliamentary Debates: Parliament of India: Official Report, Government of India Press, New Delhi, 1950–51. 16 vols.

Preventive Detention Act, No. IV of 1950 (As modified up to the 1st November, 1952), Government of India Press, New Delhi, 1952. 6 pp.

Report of the Press Commission, Part I, Government of India Press, New Delhi, 1954. vi, 538 pp.

E. Unpublished Materials

Townsley, Hendrix Atkinson, 'An Investigation of the Philosophy of Jawaharlal Nehru with Particular Emphasis on his Philosophy of Religion'. Unpublished Master of Theology thesis, The University of Southern California, Los Angeles, 1949.

F. Newspapers

The Hindu (Madras), 1946-55.

The New York Times, September 22, 1950.

The Times of India (Bombay and New Delhi), 1946-55.

INDEX

A

Allahabad, 11, 15
Anarchists, 78
Arthashastra, 49-50
Assumptions of the study, 4; basis for, 4-8
Aurobindo, 183

B

Balance, concept of, 63, 136, 179-81
Bentham, Jeremy, 43
Besant, Mrs. Annie, 13
Biographical data on Nehru:
childhood, 11-12; education, 12-13; first political activities, 13-14; marriage, 14; experience with the peasants, 14; in non-co-operation movement, 14-15; Gandhi's influence during early 1920s, 15; 1926 visit to Europe and influence of socialism, 15-17; Congress and trade-union activities, 18; writings during prison terms of early 1930s, 19-24, 77; death of his wife, 26; 1936 address to Congress, 26-8; series of disappointments, 29-30; disillusionment with U.S.S.R., 30-1; *The Discovery of India*, 32-5; Interim Government formed, 36; independence and drafting of Constitution, 36-7; major developments in his political thought since 1947, 37-9
Boer War, 12
Bowles, Chester:
on importance of Nehru's thought, quotation coming before the Preface; on Nehru's frankness, 6; on his contribution to the secular state, 149; on land reform in India, 132-3
Brooks, Ferdinand T., 12

C

Campbell-Johnson, Alan, 9
Cambridge University, 12
Capitalism:
Nehru's attitude toward, 22, 59, 113, 120; relation to imperialism, 20-1, 26-7; opposed to democracy, 20, 59-60; greatly modified today, 105, 124; choice between it and socialism, 104-5, 120-1
Caste system:
and democracy, 50, 60-1; threat to the secular state, 151-2, 166-70

Centralization, 48-9, 124-5
Chinese thought, 33
Civil code, uniform, 162-6
Class struggle, 22, 64, 105-6
Classless society, 60, 64, 105, 107
Collectivism, 124-5
Commonwealth of Nations, 37
Communalism, 3, 24, 75, 79, 89-91, 150-2, 172; and Muslim League, 7, 29, 36, 155
Communism, 16, 22-4, 26-8, 34, 43, 46, 73, 110; *see also* Marxism, Socialism
Communist Party of India, 78-9
Compromises, need for, 58
Compulsory acquisition of land, 133-45
Conclusions of the study:
characteristic emphases of Nehru's thought, 177-81; Nehru as a political thinker, 181-3
Conflict and balance, concept of, 63, 136, 179-81
Congress, Indian National:
joined by Nehru, 13; meets Gandhi at Lucknow Congress, 13; Nehru General Secretary of, 14; Nehru President of, 18, 28; resolutions of Karachi Congress, 19, 52, 73-4, 78, 150; address to Lucknow Congress, 26-8; Gandhi's arbitrary rule over, 29; leadership within, 8; rejects Government of India Act of 1935, 28; passes Quit India resolution, 32; and co-operation with Praja Socialists, 55; 1951 Election Manifesto, 124, 152; Avadi Congress, 130-1
Congress of Oppressed Nationalities, 16
Consistency, test of, 5-6
Constitution of India:
work in Constituent Assembly, 36-8, 44-5, 50, 161-2; Objectives resolution, 38, 45-6, 110; conflict between Directive Principles and Fundamental Rights, 60, 62-3, 140-1; constitutional basis of secular state, 52, 157-9; article 15, 168-9; article 19, 92-6; article 31, 135-41; article 42, 163; First Amendment Bill, 62, 93-6, 168-9; Fourth Amendment Bill, 5, 141, 144
Constitution of Pakistan, 150, 152-3, 159
Cottage industries, 128
Cow slaughter controversy, 6-7, 170-2
Cripps Proposals, 32

D

Dayabhaga school of Hindu law, 163
Delhi Agreement (Nehru-Liaquat Pact)
90-1
Delhi Pact, 19
Democracy:
sources of Nehru's ideas about it,
37-8, 43, 74; in ancient Indian traditions, 19, 45, 49-50, 65; in relation
to socialism, 19-20, 37-8, 47, 51, 59-
60, 106-7; deeper probing of its
meaning since independence, 37-8;
various definitions of, 44, 59, 61,
66-7; defined as individual freedom,
45-9, 71-80, 91-2; defined as representative institutions, 49-59; as
economic and social equality, 59-63,
108-14; as social self-discipline, 63-5,
75-7, 91-2; related to freedom and
equality, 61-3; related to freedom
and order, 47-8; related to political
leadership, 54-8; related to freedom
and centralization, 48-9, 125-6; as
government by the unthinking
masses, 45, 53-4; versus totalitar-
ianism, 46-7, 120; summary of
Nehru's definitions of, 66-7
Dewey, John, 29
Dharma, 65
Directive Principles of State Policy, 60,
62-3, 110, 140-1, 167, 170
Discovery of India, ideas of, 28, 32-5

E

Economic democracy:
as an ideal, 59-63, 108-14; economic
equality one aspect of, 108-12; co-
operative effort replacing profit
motive, 112-14; summary of Nehru's
views on, 114-15; *see also* Democracy,
Socialism
Eisenhower, Dwight D., 3, 8
Elections:
essential to democracy, 50-1, 53-4;
general elections of 1951-52, 37, 56;
separate communal electorates, 159-
62
England, influence on Nehru, 13
Equality, *see* Democracy, Socialism,
Economic democracy

F

Fabians, 13, 101-2
Fascism, 26, 46
Five Year Plan, 117, 121, 129
Freedom, individual, (*see* Fundamental
rights, Democracy, Individual)
Fundamental rights:
basis in Indian traditions, 19, 45-6;
Karachi resolutions on, 19, 52, 73-4,

78, 150; conflict with Directive Principles, 60, 62-3; background of
Nehru's conception of, 71-5; Nehru's
basic approach to, 75-7; regarding
personal liberty, 77-80; and the
Preventive Detention Act, 80-84;
and freedom of the press, 84-96; and
Article 19 of the Constitution, 92-6;
summary of Nehru's views on, 96-7;
criticism of Nehru's views on, 84

G

Gandhi, Mohandas K.:
Nehru's first meeting with, 13; influence on Nehru during 1920s, 15;
during 1930s, 24-6; withdraws civil
disobedience, 26; his decisions imposed on Congress, 29; his ideas on
democracy, 183; his ideas on socialism, 25; his ideas on industrialization,
15, 25; influence on Nehru regarding peaceful methods, 58, 65; emphasized individual salvation not
society, 25, 113; his ideas on land
reform, 25, 133; influence on Nehru
regarding secular state, 154-7; his
veneration for the cow, 170
Garibaldi, 12
Government of India Act, 28, 74
Glimpses of World History, ideas of,
19-24

H

Harijan Welfare Departments, 167-70
Harrow, 12
Hart, Liddell, 58
Hindu Code Bill, 163-6
Hindu law, 151, 162-6
Hindu Mahasabha, 4, 24, 172
Humanism, in Nehru's philosophy,
33-5, 38, 71

I

Imperialism, *see* Nationalism
Individual, the:
modern process of de-individualization, 45, 53-4; freedom necessary for
development of, 45-7, 49, 71-2, 75-6;
and need for eradicating the profit
motive, 112-14
Industrial Policy, Resolution on, 128-30
Industrial Revolution, effect on political life, 53, 86
Internationalism, 21-2, 28-9

J

Jagirdars, 78-80, see also *Zamindari*
system
Jan Sangh, 4, 172
Jinnah, M. A., 29

Judiciary, Nehru's attitude toward, 81-3, 136-7, 139, 144-5

K

Kamala Nehru:
marriage to Nehru, 14; death, 26
Karachi resolutions on Fundamental Rights and Duties, 19, 52, 73-4, 78, 150
Kazi, Syed Karimuddin, resolution of, 105, 131
Khadi, 128
Krushchev, 3

L

Ladejinsky, Wolf, quoted on India's land problem, 133
Laissez-faire, 124
Landlordism, 131-4
Land reform:
Lucknow Congress resolution on, 133; Nehru's views on, 5, 133-43; criticism of Nehru's views, 143-5
Laski, Harold J., 20, 102
Lenin, 16, 22-3, 26-8, 34, 101-3
Locke, John, 43

M

Macmillan, Harold, 8
Majority rule:
basic to democracy, 51-3; limited by rights of minorities, 52
Mao Tse-tung, 3
Marxism, 16, 22-4, 26-8, 34, 43, 101-4, 119-20; *see also* Socialism, Communism
Mill, John Stuart, 43, 71-2
Mitakshara school of Hindu law, 163
Mixed economy, 39, 105, 119-29
Mollet, Guy, 8
Montagu-Chelmsford Report, 161
Montesquieu, 43, 73
Mookherjee, H. C., 162
Mountbatten, Lord, 36
Muslim League, 7, 29, 36, 155

N

Narain, Jai Prakash:
organized Congress Socialist Party 24; on the goal of socialism, 6, 111-12
Nasser, 3
Nationalism 7, 13, 15, 17-18, 20-1, 102; in relation to internationalism, 21-2, 27, 38
Nationalization of industry, 122-3, 127
Nazism, 23, 26, 46
Nehru, Motilal, 11, 19, 25

O

Ortega y Gasset, José, 45, 53

P

Pakistan, India's relations with, 36-7, 90-1, 95-6
Patel, Sardar Vallabhbhai, 8
Peasants, problems of, 14, 103, 131-4
Planning, 107, 117, 121; National Planning Committee, 29; Planning Commission, 124, 126; *see also* Five Year Plan
Political parties:
Nehru's criticism of England's party system, 54; criticism of Nehru's views on, 55-6
Political theory and the politician, 4-8, 56-8
Pragmatism in Nehru's thought, 23, 35, 39, 119-22
Press, freedom of, 84-5; modern conditions relating to, 85-91; report of the Press Commission, 85-91; in relation to Article 19, 92-6; summary of Nehru's views on, 96-7
Preventive Detention Act, 80-4
Private Sector, 123-9
Production, importance of, 39, 106, 122-3, 142-3
Profit motive, 112-14
Property:
conception of, 137-8; right of, 7, 141, 145

R

Religion, Nehru's views on, 12, 15, 23, 33, 156
Rights of Man, Declaration of, 47
Rosenthal, A. M., 3
Rousseau, 43
Rowlatt Act, 14
Russell, Bertrand, 14, 29
Russia, Soviet, Nehru's attitude toward, 5, 16-17, 27-8, 30-1, 46-7, 73, 104, 119-20
Russo-Japanese War, 12

S

Sabine, George H., quoted in Preface
Salt Act, 18
Satyagraha, 14-15, 18, 65
Scientific method, 12, 23-4, 35, 38-9, 102-3, 119
Secular state:
Nehru's contribution toward, 149, 172-3; definition of, 149-53; essential in modern times, 153-4; Gandhi on, 154-7; constitutional basis of, 157-9; and separate electorates, 159-62; and uniform civil code, 152-6; and caste, 166-70; and cow slaughter, 170-2; summary of Nehru's views on, 173-4

Separate electorates, 159-62
Shaw, George Bernard, 101-2
Socialism:
  Nehru's early attraction to, 13-14, 97;
  closer contact with in Europe, 16-7;
  exposition of in *Glimpses of World
  History*, 22-3; Gandhi's socialism, 25;
  Nehru's devotion to principles of,
  27-8, 59-60; his adherence to dis-
  turbed, 31; modification of Nehru's
  socialism, 38-9, 104-8; sources of
  Nehru's socialism, 101-4; comparison
  of Nehru's socialism, 1935 and 1955,
  104-8; *see also* Marxism
Socialistic pattern of society, 108,
  129-31
Sources of Nehru's democratic thought,
  37-8, 43
Sovereignty, popular, 49-50, 53-4
Spanish Civil War, its effect on Nehru,
  28-9
Sun Yat-sen, 183

T

Tagore, Rabindranath, 34, 183
Talukdari system, 133; see also *Zamindari* system

Tawney, R. H., 102
Theories, value of, 120-1
Theosophy, 12
Tilak, 12-13
Tito, Marshal, 3
Tolerance, 64, 72
Townsend, Meredith, 12
Trade-Union Congress, 18

U

Untouchability, efforts to eradicate,
  167-70
Utilitarians, 52

V

Vivekananda, 183

W

Wavell, Lord, 36
Webb, Sidney, 101-2
Welfare state, 111

Z

Zamindari system, 131-4; Gandhi's
  defence of, 25